COMMERCE DEFENDED

Also Published in

Reprints of Economic Classics

By James Mill

Elements of Political Economy [1844]

COMMERCE DEFENDED

By

JAMES MILL

[1808]

REPRINTS OF ECONOMIC CLASSICS

AUGUSTUS M. KELLEY, BOOKSELLER
NEW YORK 1965

Library of Congress Catalogue Card Number
65 - 19652

COMMERCE DEFENDED.

AN

ANSWER TO THE ARGUMENTS

BY WHICH

MR. SPENCE, MR. COBBETT,

AND OTHERS,

HAVE ATTEMPTED TO PROVE THAT

Commerce

IS NOT A

SOURCE OF NATIONAL WEALTH.

———◆———

BY JAMES MILL, Esq.

Author of an Essay on the Impolicy of a Bounty on the Exportation
of Corn.

———◆———

London :

PRINTED FOR C. AND R. BALDWIN, NEW BRIDGE-STREET.

———

1808.

Price Four Shillings.

CONTENTS.

COMMERCE DEFENDED,

&c. &c.

INTRODUCTION.

ROUSSEAU confessed to Mr. Hume, and Mr. Hume repeated the conversation to Mr. Burke, that the secret of which he availed himself in his writings to excite the attention of mankind, was the employment of paradoxes. When a proposition is so expressed as to bear the appearance of absurdity, but by certain reasonings and explanations is made to assume the semblance of truth, the inexperienced hearers are, in general, wonderfully delighted, give credit to the author for the highest ingenuity, and congratulate themselves on a surprising discovery.

When these paradoxes are so contrived as to harmonize with any prevailing sentiment or passion of the times, their reception is so much the more eager and general. Thus, had the paradox, that commerce is absolutely unproductive of wealth, been recommended to the people of this country some years ago, when they were taught to triumph in the increase of their commerce, and to look to it as the means of humbling the revolutionary pride of France, it would have been the object either of neglect or of ridicule. At pre-

B

sent, when difficulties and dangers have encreased around this commerce, and fears are abroad that it may even be cut off, the new doctrine that we shall not suffer by its loss, falls in so conveniently with our apprehensions, that it appears extremely agreeable and consolatory. Being a doctrine at once paradoxical and flattering, no more is wanting to render it popular.

It is to be suspected, however, that this would not afford a very safe principle on which to regulate the great interests of the nation. Our navy, for example, weighty as its ascendancy must be deemed, may now, when the whole continent of civilized Europe is at the disposal of its determined enemy, be regarded as exposed to dangers, greater, perhaps, than ever threatened it before. Could we, in a moment of despondency, permit ourselves to think, that, like our commerce, it might be ruined by this enemy, should our wisdom consist in trying to persuade ourselves that it was of no value, and that we ought to part from it without regret? Ireland, too, considering the power of the enemy who desires to attack it, and the commotions by which it is agitated within, is unquestionably in greater danger of being wrested from us at this moment, than at any late period of our history. What then? Should we consider any man as acting a patriotic or prudent part, who should labour to persuade us that Ireland is of little or no value, and should it fall into the hands of Bonaparte, that the loss we should sustain would be of little avail? We should, on the other hand, join in condemning his misguided and preposterous zeal; for however we might rest assured that neither Ireland nor our navy would be voluntarily, any more than our commerce, resigned to Bonaparte, yet we might fear that such a doctrine becoming popular would induce our Cabinets and Parliaments, which are not always led by the wisest men in the nation, to neglect those essential interests more than they otherwise would have done.

This is precisely the danger which threatens commerce at the present moment, and which is the more alarming, the greater the difficulties by which it is surrounded, and the more delicate and easily affected the interests which it involves. Agriculture is hardy and independent. The powers of the earth, and the first necessities of man, insure to this a certain prosperity, proportionate to the state of industry in the nation, in spite of the neglect, and even the discouragement of the public rulers. But should the legislature become influenced by a theory hostile to commerce, at a time when other circumstances conspire against it, the affairs of the nation might easily receive a turn, which would soon terminate her grandeur as the mistress of trade.

The propagators of this doctrine, which has met with a more favourable reception in this commercial country than beforehand one could have easily imagined, are, as yet, but two, Mr. Spence and Mr. Cobbett.

Mr. Spence has written a pamphlet, in which, after exhibiting in as high colours as he possibly can the value which is vulgarly set upon commerce in this country, he endeavours to shew that it will certainly, or at least very probably, be torn from us by Bonaparte; that it is however altogether destitute of value; and that our wealth and prosperity are intrinsic. To establish these conclusions Mr. Spence attempts to revive the system of the *Economistes*, a sect of political philosophers who arose in France about the middle of the last century, and who, in opposition to the mercantile doctrine, that all wealth is derived from commerce, or rather a favourable balance of commerce, taught that all wealth is derived from land. He proposes indeed a limitation upon the ideas of that sect, in one particular instance, from which however he seems to waver in other parts of his discourse; but the main object of the pamphlet, as he expressly states, is to apply the doctrine of the *Economistes* to the present circumstances of this country. Mr. Spence appears from his pamphlet to have a considerable turn for abstract thinking, and to be a man of pretty extensive reading in political economy. But his mind has not been trained in the logic of enlarged and comprehensive views. He does not judge of an extensive and complicated subject from an exact knowledge of all its parts, of their various connections, and relative importance. It is enough for him to seize some leading object, or some striking relation, and from these to draw conclusions with ingenuity to the whole.

Mr. Cobbett is an author who deals more in

assertion than proof; and therefore a writer who gives reasons for what Mr. Cobbett affirms, is a very convenient coadjutor. He seems, accordingly, to have been charmed with the appearance of Mr. Spence's pamphlet; and has republished the principal part of that gentleman's reasonings, in his Political Register. Even the assertions of Mr. Cobbett, I am by no means disposed to treat with neglect. He seems to form his opinions more frequently from a sort of intuition, than from argument. His mind is but little accustomed to spread out, as it were, before itself, the intermediate ideas on which its conclusions are founded; and the nature of the education which it has received, from its own unaided progress and exertions, sufficiently accounts for this peculiarity. It does not follow that his opinions are not founded on evidence, and that they do not frequently exhibit much sagacity. It is often the form, rather than the matter, in which he is deficient. Even on some pretty difficult questions of political economy, (those, for example, respecting the corn-trade,) he has discovered a clearness and justness of thought, which but few of our scientific reasoners have reached. On a subject, more perverted at least by passion, the structure of society, his mind, untainted by theory, or rather emancipated by its own vigour and honesty from a pernicious theory which it had imbibed, has seized the doctrines of wisdom and prosperity, without the aid of many examples. He has assumed the patronage of the poor, at a time when they are depressed below the place which they have fortunately held in this country for a century, and when the current of our policy runs to depress them still farther. At a time, too, when every tongue and every pen seem formed to adulation, when nothing is popular but praises of men in power, and whatever tendency to corruption may exist receives in this manner double encouragement, he has the courage boldly to arraign the abuses of government and the vices of the great. This is a distinction which, with all his defects, ranks him among the most eminent of his countrymen.

Such are the two authors whose doctrines, respecting the value of commerce, have at present attained no little celebrity; and whose reasonings it will be a principal part of our business, in the following pages, to examine.

CHAPTER I.

On the Security or Insecurity of the British Commerce.

BOTH of these Authors preface their inquiries into the value of commerce, by an attempt to persuade us that the commerce of this country has become extremely insecure. This is not exactly the most philosophical course, as it is taking aid from our fears in support of their argument. Mr. Spence informs us,* that ' the ' idea which a few years ago would have been ' laughed at, that any man could acquire the ' power of shutting the whole continent against ' our trade, seems now not unlikely to be rea- ' lized.' And Mr. Cobbett assures us, that the soldier is abroad, and will not return home till he hath acquired a share of the good things of the world. On this point, those two champions appear to be at variance. The soldier will certainly not get possession of any of our good things, by shutting them out from the Continent; and if he

* " Britain Independent of Commerce," p. 7. It is necessary here to remark, that as nearly the whole of the present Tract was written before the 3d edition of Mr. Spence's pamphlet appeared, it is the 2d edition always that is quoted, unless when the 3d edition is actually named.

comes and takes them, we shall be in danger of losing our land as well as our commerce.

A calm and rational view of our circumstances, will probably soon convince us that neither the one bugbear of these authors, nor the other, ought in the highest degree to alarm us; and that it will be only by our own egregious misconduct, if we suffer any considerable disaster, from the efforts of our enemy either to invade us or to destroy our commerce. In regard to invasion, the experiment may be said to have been fairly tried, and to have failed; in the vast preparations made by Bonaparte, and the abandonment of the attempt to employ them. This danger then, especially as it seems to have little influence at present on the public feelings, we may pass without further notice. The experiment of excluding our commerce is now to be tried, and it may be regarded as a fortunate circumstance, that it can be tried so completely. When our enemy is thoroughly convinced, that neither his invading nor his excluding scheme, can be made the instrument of any serious injury to us; and when we ourselves are convinced that we have nothing either in peace or war to fear from him, the minds of both parties may decidedly incline to peace.

Let us only contemplate for one moment the vast extent of the habitable globe, and consider how small in comparison is that portion of coast over which the sway of Bonaparte extends; and we shall probably conclude with considerable confidence, that in the wide world channels will be found for all the commerce, to which this little island can administer. Let us look first at the United States of America. To these, we have for years sent more goods of British manufacture than to the whole continent of Europe. The vast commerce of the West India Islands, next comes naturally in view. The immense extent of Portuguese and Spanish America, whose communication with manufacturing countries, may in a great measure be confined to ourselves, will, notwithstanding the disadvantages under which they labour, furnish a growing demand for the produce of our industry. Even the coasts of Africa, miserable as their condition is, might present to the careful explorer something better for the commodities which he may offer, than their wretched population. The Cape of Good Hope itself, improved by British wisdom and British capital, opens a field of boundless extent. The vast shores of the Indian ocean, both continental and insular, with their unrivalled productions, are all our own. Whatever the ingenuity of the Indian, the Malay, and the Chinese can produce, or their various and productive soils can yield, is ready to be exchanged for the commodities which we can supply to the wants of that immense population.

This superficial review can hardly fail to satisfy the man, who knows but the outline of geography, that, while Britain is mistress of the sea, she might have scope for a boundless commerce, though the whole continent of Europe were swallowed up by an earthquake. But in regard to Europe itself, it is only to the superficial eye,

that the power of Bonaparte over our commerce
can appear important. Not to mention the probability that the Baltic, the channel by which a
great part of our commerce has for a number
of years found its way into Europe, will not long
be shut against us ; the very notion of guarding
the whole extent of European coast, from the
mouth of the Elbe to the gulph of Venice, must
appear ridiculous to all men of information and
reflection. Let any man but consider the well
known fact, that under the very eye of the most
vigilant Custom House in the world, and where
an actual army of Custom House officers is concentrated, contraband East India goods are regularly contracted for by the smugglers, to be
delivered in any house in London, for 25 per
cent. Even Hollands and brandy, which are not
the most handy commodities, are currently landed
in the Downs, in the presence of a British fleet.
With a knowledge of these facts, can it be supposed, that any British goods which the Continent
wants, will not find their way into it in spite of
any regulations which Bonaparte can adopt? A
line of soldiers regularly planted from one ex-
tremity of the coast to another, from the point
of Jutland to the bottom of the Adriatic gulph,
would not suffice to exclude our commerce.

An important fact is to be considered. The
population of Great Britain take no interest in
the success of the smugglers. The greater or
at least the superior part condemn the traffic, and
rather wish to obstruct it. The case is very different on the Continent. Even in France, the

great mass of the people wish for British commodities, and condemn the policy which excludes them. But in what may be called the conquered countries, in Holland for example, and Portugal, the interests and the ancient habits of the people of all ranks, give them the strongest propensity to elude, by every possible contrivance, the restrictive policy of Bonaparte. Where a whole people have the strongest interest in deceiving the government, in a case in which it can be so easily deceived as in the exclusion of British commerce from the Continent, we may confidently conclude that the public decrees will be very indifferently executed. If 25 per cent. can cover the expence of smuggling in the Downs, we may be certain that one half of that sum will be sufficient to cover the expence of smuggling British goods on the coasts of Europe. Even from this expence are to be deducted the Custom House duties which must have been paid in the course of regular entry; so that in many cases British goods will reach the continental consumer, loaded with an expence of probably not more than 5 per cent. above what they would have cost in the way of regular trade. But allowing their price to be enhanced at a rate of 10 or 12 per cent., the deduction which this can occasion from the quantity which would otherwise be sold, cannot bear a very great proportion to the general amount of the extensive, various, and unrivalled traffic of Great Britain.

The fact is, the British commerce has much more to fear from the injudicious regulations of the British government, than from the decrees of Bonaparte. The great instrument of that species of traffic, which must now be carried on with the Continent, are neutral bottoms. It will not be very difficult, however, for our ministers to put it out of the power of the neutrals to serve us in this important capacity. The late orders of council are of a nature to give effect to the decrees of Bonaparte, beyond any thing which the plenitude of his power could achieve. Instead of thwarting and restricting the intercourse of neutrals, Britain ought studiously to afford it every facility and accommodation. Wherever a neutral vessel obtains admittance into a continental port, means are afforded for introducing British goods. If the orders of the British council however serve to unveil the disguises, under which the neutrals might be enabled to cover our goods, this important resource may be in a great measure cut off, and the ingenuity of the merchants, so fertile in expedients for eluding the restrictions on trade, may be defeated.—We may perceive then, in the wide extent of the world, and its innumerable productions and wants, in our dominion of the seas, and in the impotence of all exclusive efforts, sufficient security for our commerce, if we exercise but common prudence, in spite of all external hostilities that can be waged against it.

CHAP. II.

On Land, as a Source of Wealth.

IN the praises which the *Economistes*, together with Mr. Spence and Mr. Cobbett, bestow upon land as a source of wealth, absolutely considered, the intelligent reader will not hesitate to join. Of all species of labour, that which is bestowed upon the soil, is in general rewarded by the most abundant product. In the present circumstances of the greater part of Europe, the cultivation of the soil not only pays the wages of labour, and the profit of stock employed in it, the sole return of other species of industry, but over and above this affords a share of the produce payable as rent to the landlord. On this point, therefore, no controversy strictly exists ; and when the patrons of the agricultural theory lament that the cabinets and legislatures of Europe, influenced by the ideas of the mercantile system, have so often thrown obstructions in the way of rural industry in favour of manufactures and trade, we acknowledge the justness of their accusations. One of the main objects which the immortal Smith proposed to himself, was to unfold the delusions of the mercantile system, by which the policy of almost all the governments of Europe was turned to the encouragement of trade rather than of agriculture, and a greater share of the industry and capital of every nation than consisted with its interests, was thus forcibly diverted into the commercial channel. Even to this hour the sound inquirer has most frequently occasion for his efforts in exposing the errors into which both governments and individuals fall by the remaining influence of the same theory. The firm hold indeed which this doctrine yet maintains on the minds of men, forms the principal obstacle to the diffusion, among mankind, of juster principles of political economy and of government. When a system, therefore, is propagated, diametrically opposite to the Mercantile, we might quietly allow the two theories to combat one another; and trust that the exposure of errors, if not the establishment of truths, would be the consequence. Unfortunately, however, it is much more the propensity of mankind to run from one extreme into another, than to rest in the wise and salutary middle ; and a bias to the errors of the agricultural system would be not a whit less pernicious than a bias to the system which it would supplant. Of this indeed we have experimental proof; as some of the worst regulations which the new legislators of France adopted, were entirely founded upon the system of the *Economistes.*

There is one consequence of the doctrine which Messrs. Spence and Cobbett have embraced, which they seem rather unfairly to have kept out of sight. They address themselves with great industry to the self-interest of the landholders, and study to win their support by representing the landed interest as deeply affected by the opinions which they wish to subvert. They abstain, however, from informing this class of their readers, that land, according to their doctrine, is the one and only proper subject of taxation. This the Economistes taught. It is a logical conclusion from their principles. If land be the one and only source of wealth, the absurdity is evident of seeking in any other quarter that portion of the national produce which is required for the necessities of the state; nor can one single argument be used against the exclusive taxation of land, which is not an argument, equally pointed, against the doctrine which the agricultural theorists espouse. It is shrewdly to be suspected that the landholders would deem themselves but little indebted to those gentlemen for the establishment of their system, if it was to be followed by this practical consequence. The fact is, that land in this country bears infinitely less than its due proportion of taxes, while commerce is loaded with them. At the beginning of the last century, and previous to that period, the land-tax equalled, or rather exceeded, the whole amount of all the other taxes taken together. How insignificant a proportion does the land-tax now bear to the taxes on consumable commodities? The land-tax has remained without augmentation, while the permanent taxes have risen from little more than two millions to upwards of two and forty millions a year, and while the value of land has risen from fourteen or fifteen years purchase to thirty years purchase and upwards. The landholders, therefore, have little foundation for complaining, though the policy of the country has frequently appeared to favour mercantile rather than agricultural industry. By their superior influence in the legislature, they have taken care to repay themselves, as far as their personal interests were concerned, by throwing the burthen of the taxes upon the growing produce of commerce, while the increasing value of land stood exempt. The interests, however, of the country at large, the interests of the middling and industrious classes, have thus suffered in two ways. They have suffered by sustaining an undue proportion of the taxes; and they have suffered by the diminution of the annual produce of the land and labour of the country.*

* Mr. Spence, in a new passage inserted in his 3d edition, p 40. does at last state it as a consequence of his doctrine, ' that all taxes, however levied, in the end fall upon the soil.' But this is very different from saying that they ought to be immediately levied upon the soil. The landholders may very quietly allow you to say that the taxes *fall* upon them, as long as you make them *light* upon others. Mr. Spence is even accommodating enough to say that the corollary of the *Economistes* is wrong; and that taxes ought not to light, as they teach, upon the landlords. It is matter of regret he did not give us his reasons; for I can discover none which are not as strong against the theory as against the corollary. Unfortunately, however, all that Mr. Spence affords us on this score is the following;—' Reasons,' says he, (Ibid, p. 41, 42,) ' which it is impracticable in this plan to ' adduce, render it doubtful, whether a direct land-tax would

1

CHAP. III.

Of the Definition of the Terms Wealth and Prosperity.

MR. Spence, with a view to introduce accuracy into his inquiry, presents us near the commencement of his pamphlet with a definition of the terms Wealth and Prosperity. This was indeed highly necessary, for while our ideas waver on this point, all our reasonings, respecting the wealth and prosperity of nations, must by consequence be uncertain and deceitful. It is of the utmost importance, therefore, in the examination of Mr. Spence's doctrines, to ascertain the precision or inaccuracy of his definition of wealth. The following passage contains not only the definition but its illustration:

* ' In investigating the present subject, it will be
' necessary previously to inquire into the opinions
' which have been held relative to the real sources
' of wealth and prosperity to a nation, and we
' shall then be able to apply the results deduced
' from such an examination to our own case. And

' be advisable even in an infant state; and it is much more
' obvious that the intricate and artificial regulations of
' adult societies wholly preclude the propriety of such a
' tax.'

* See pp. 9, 10.

' in the first place, the meaning of the terms,
' wealth and prosperity, must be settled; for, if
' the reader were to take these words in their
' usual acceptation, if he were to conclude, that
' by the first is meant gold and silver merely, and
' by the latter extensive dominion, powerful ar-
' mies, &c. he would be affixing to these terms
' meanings very different from those which are
' here meant to be annexed to them, and ideas,
' which, however common, are founded in error.
' Spain has plenty of gold and silver, yet she has
' no wealth; whilst Britain is wealthy with scarcely
' a guinea: and France, with her numerous con-
' quests, her extended influence, and her vast ar-
' mies, is probably not enjoying much prosperity;
' certainly not nearly so much as we enjoy, though
' we have far less influence, and much smaller ar-
' mies than she has. Wealth, then, is defined to
' consist in abundance of capital, of cultivated
' and productive land, and of those things which
' man usually esteems valuable. Thus, a country
' where a large proportion of inhabitants have ac-
' cumulated fortunes; where much of the soil is
' productively cultivated, and yields a considerable
' revenue to the land-owner, may be said to be
' wealthy; and on the contrary, a nation where
' few of the inhabitants are possessed of property,
' and where the land is badly cultivated, and yields
' but little revenue to the proprietor, may be truly
' said to be poor. Britain is an example of the
' first state, Spain and Italy of the last. A na-
' tion may be said to be in prosperity, which is
' progressively advancing in wealth, where the

' checks to population are few, and where em-
' ployment and subsistence are readily found for all
' classes of its inhabitants. It does not follow,
' that a prosperous nation must be wealthy ; thus
' America, though enjoying great prosperity, has
' not accumulated wealth. Nor does it follow,
' that because a nation possesses wealth, it is there-
' in a state of prosperity. All those symptoms
' of wealth which have been enumerated, may
' exist, and yet a nation may in prosperity be
' going retrograde, its wealth may be stationary,
' its population kept at a stand, and the difficulty
' of getting employment for those who seek it,
' may be becoming greater and greater every day.'

First, here, Mr. Spence warns us against supposing that wealth consists in gold and silver merely,
and that prosperity consists in extensive dominion,
powerful armies, and the like; and assuredly if
any one entertains this idea of wealth and prosperity, he is in a woeful delusion. Having learned
from Mr. Spence what wealth and prosperity are
not, let us next learn what they are. ' Wealth,'
he says, ' is defined to consist in abundance of
' capital, of cultivated and productive land, and of
' those things which man usually esteems valu-
' able.' Here three things are enumerated as the
constituents of wealth. The first is capital. Now
it is an established and indispensible rule in definition, that the words themselves in which the definition is conceived should be of the most precise
and determinate signification; because, otherwise,
the definition is of no use. But here the term
' capital' stands as much in need of definition as the

term wealth, which it is brought to define. What is capital, or wherein does it consit? There are as many difficulties in these questions, as in the questions, What is wealth, and wherein does it consist? To define one vague and ambiguous word by another which is equally vague and ambiguous, is to pay us with mere words instead of ideas. The second constituent of wealth, according to Mr. Spence's definition, is cultivated and productive land. But would not Mr. Spence allow that uncultivated land, if it might be very easily cultivated and rendered productive, ought also to be accounted wealth? In a definition where every thing ought to be in the highest degree accurate, an exception even of this sort is important. Let us, however, attend particularly to what Mr. Spence states as the third constituent of wealth ; ' Those things which man usually ' esteems valuable.' This is a sweeping clause. In the first place this third constituent includes both the other two, for undoubtedly capital and productive land are among the things which man esteems valuable. The third constituent, therefore, is not only the third, but the first, second, and third all in one.* It would have been much better without enumerating the first two, which are undoubtedly but parts of the last, to have said at once that wealth consisted in those things which man usually esteems valuable. Still, how-

* This is just such a definition, as if, describing the corporal part of man, we should say that it consisted of a trunk, limbs, and body.

ever, the expression would have been so vague as to be entirely useless as a definition. Man usually esteems air and light as very valuable, but in what sense can they be regarded as national wealth ? It is very evident from this explanation that Mr. Spence neither understands what is requisite to a definition, nor has formed to himself any distinct idea of the meaning of the term wealth.

Another particularity in this definition is worthy of a little attention. Mr. Spence says that wealth is defined to consist in *abundance* of capital, &c. When Mr. Spence, or any other political philosopher, inquires whether land, or manufactures, or commerce be the source of wealth, the question is not respecting quantity. We say that land is productive of wealth, without considering whether the quantity be one bushel or a million. But when Mr. Spence defines wealth as consisting in *abundance* of capital, land, and valuable things, he evidently confounds the philosophical meaning of the word with the vulgar, in which wealth signifies a great quantity of riches. So much for Mr. Spence's definition of wealth.

Let us next consider what he says in regard to prosperity. He does not indeed attempt to define prosperity; but he gives us a description of a nation which may be said to be in prosperity. ' It is a nation which is progressively advancing ' in wealth, where the checks to population are ' few, and where employment and subsistence are ' readily found for all classes of its inhabitants. It would be tedious here to enter into the same

minute analysis which we applied to the definition of wealth. We may barely remark, that of
the three clauses of which the description consists,
the last two are included in the first; as it is in
the nation which is progressively advancing in
wealth where the checks to population are few-
est, and where employment and subsistence are
most readily found for all classes of the inhabitants. This indeed is neither more nor less than
the circumstance which is so well illustrated by
Dr. Smith in the Wealth of Nations, B. I. c. 8.

Having seen how little useful are the defini-
tions with which Mr. Spence has favoured us, it
will be necessary for our subsequent inquiries to
explain accurately in what sense the term wealth
will there be used; and as this is the subject on
which we are at present engaged, no other place
can be more proper for the explanation. Wealth
is relative to the term value; it is necessary therefore first to affix a meaning to the latter. The
term value has in common acceptation two meanings. It signifies either value in use, or value in
exchange. Thus water has great value in use but
commonly has no value in exchange, that is to
say, nothing can be obtained for it in purchase.
On the other hand, a diamond or a ruby has little
or no value in use, but great value in exchange.
Now the term wealth will always be employed
in the following pages as denoting objects which
have a value in exchange, or at least notice will
be given if we have ever occasion to use it in another sense.

CHAP. IV.

Of Manufactures.

IT is at this point that our controversy with Messrs. Spence and Cobbett properly begins. They assert that manufactures are no source of wealth.* We say that they are. It is the reader's part to compare our reasons. Mr. Spence, who seems to supply the arguments of the party, says that manufactures are productive of no wealth, because the manufacturer in the preparation of

---

* 'Whether,' says Mr. Spence, (p. 19, Brit. Indep. of Commerce) ' the manufacturer receives the price of his ma-
' nufacture in food or in money, if the whole be fairly ana-
' lyzed, and every thing traced to its source, it will in every
' case be found, in the most refined, as in the most barbarous,
' state of society, that agriculture is the great source, *manufac-*
' *tures no source at all, of national wealth.*' This indeed is the hinge on which the main part of his doctrine turns. It is the foundation, for example, of his opinions concerning consumption ; and he introduces his inquiry into that subject in the following terms ; ' As it has been shewn' (see pp. 29, 30, of his pamphlet) ' that the *whole revenue* of a country, (deducting
' an insignificant portion sometimes derived from foreign com-
' merce) is derived from *its land.*' This reservation, in favour of commerce of export, he expressly denies to manufactures for home consumption. ' When a lace manufacturer,' (Ibid. p. 43) ' has been so long employed in the manufacturing a
' pound of flax into lace, that his subsistence during that period
' has cost £30, this sum is the real worth of the lace, and if it
' be sold at home, whether for £30 or £50, *the nation is no*
' *richer for this manufacture.*'

any commodity consumes a quantity of corn equal to the value which he has added to the raw materials of which the article is composed. It is to be observed, before we proceed farther, that this is the only reason which they adduce in favour of this fundamental part of their hypothesis. In this one assertion is contained the sum and substance of the evidence which they exhibit against manufactures. If this assertion is unequal to the conclusion which it is brought to support, the wonderful discoveries of the *Economistes* are on a tottering basis. I have called this fundamental proposition an assertion, because it is assumed entirely without proof, and what is more, I am afraid, in opposition to proof. When the manufacturer prepares a commodity, the prepared commodity is worth more than the food which the workmen consumed in preparing it. Do you ask my reasons? Carry it, I say, to market; you will find that it will fetch more; because it must not only repay the wages of the labour, but the profit of the stock which has been employed in its preparation. Set the goods on one side, and an equal quantity of raw materials and food with what has been consumed in their preparation on the other, and every body will give you more for the goods. The country is therefore the richer by having the goods.

Let us hear what Mr. Spence has to say in objection to this reasoning. An examination of his plea will still more clearly exhibit to us the erroneousness of his position. The superiority of price which the manufactured commodity obtains in the market, adds nothing he says to the wealth of the country; because whatever the manufacturer obtains above the value of the raw produce is taken from the landholder, the original owner of that produce. ' An example' he adds,* ' will demonstrate this: If a coach-maker were to ' employ so many men for half a year in the build- ' ing of a coach, as that for their subsistence during ' that time, he had advanced fifty quarters of corn, ' and if we suppose he sold this coach to a land ' proprietor for sixty quarters of corn, it is evi- ' dent, that the coach-maker would be ten quar- ' ters of corn richer than if he had sold it for ' fifty quarters, its original cost. But it is equally ' clear, that the land proprietor would be ten ' quarters of corn poorer, than if he had bought ' his coach at its prime cost. A transfer, then, ' not a creation of wealth, has taken place, what- ' ever one gains the other loses, and the national ' wealth is just the same.'

There is a great appearance of ingenuity and force in this reasoning; and on the greater part of mankind it is well calculated to impose. I am rather surprized, however, that a man of Mr. Spence's acuteness did not perceive that it is in reality a mere vulgar sophism. But when hypothesis has taken firm hold of a man, his acuteness is unluckily confined to one function.

Mr. Spence has here confounded two things which are remarkably different. He mistakes the sale of a coach for the manufacture of a coach. It is surely bad reasoning however to conclude

* See p. 16.

that because the sale of a coach is not productive of wealth, therefore the manufacture of a coach is not productive. The sale of the coach produces nothing; the manufacture of it however produces the coach. It is very true that when a land-holder has sixty quarters of corn and the coach-manufacturer a coach, if the coach is transferred to the landowner and the corn to the coach-maker, the country is not the richer. But it is certainly not less true that if the coach-maker has in the month of October fifty quarters of corn, which in the month of March he has transformed into a coach worth sixty quarters, the country is the richer in consequence of the manufacture of the coach, to the amount of ten bushels of corn.

Important, however, as is the addition which it thus clearly appears is made to national wealth by means of manufacturing industry, we should still have a very imperfect idea of its wonderful powers, should we confine ourselves to this observation. In a state of agriculture but moderately improved, the labourers employed in it may be regarded as raising a produce not less than five times what they themselves can consume. Were there no manufacturers, the whole of this surplus produce would be absolutely useless. Where could it find a purchaser? It is the manufacturers who convert this surplus produce into the various articles useful or agreeable to man, and who thus add the whole value it obtains to four parts at least in five of the produce of the soil.*

* It is to be borne in mind that the whole of the question discussed in this chapter respecting the utility of manufactures,

There is but one supposition, as far as I am able to perceive, by which this argument can be eluded. If our antagonists suppose a state of society in which the population has become so great that it requires the utmost efforts of the whole employed upon the land to produce food for the society; in that case they may insist that the whole produce of the soil is employed and obtains a value without the aid of manufacturers. In this state of things, however, it is unfortunate that the argument of Mr. Spence will prove not manufactures only, but land to be unproductive. The cultivators of the soil, during the time in which they raise a certain produce, have here consumed a quantity of produce of an equal value. But this is the very reason which he adduces to prove that manufactures are not a source of wealth. Manufactures then never cease to produce wealth, except in one case, in which land itself ceases to produce it; so that when manufactures cease to produce wealth, every thing ceases to produce it; wealth cannot be produced at all.— So much for Mr. Spence's reasoning against manufactures.

The truth is, that to give even tolerable plausibility to the theory of the *Economistes* we must

regards manufactures for home consumption; and, for the sake of distinctness, the idea of foreign commerce is altogether excluded. Mr. Spence has judiciously adopted this plan; and his example was here highly worthy of imitation. To know the value of manufactures it was right in the first place to consider their operation in a country supposed to have no connection with any other.

allow that nothing is useful or valuable to man but the bare necessaries of life, or rather the raw produce of the soil. If any thing else is valuable to him, whatever creates that value must add to his riches. The reasonings of the *Economistes* indeed proceed upon a most contracted and imperfect view of the operations and nature of man. How limited would be his enjoyments were he confined to the raw produce of the soil! How much are those enjoyments, how much is his wellbeing, promoted by the various productions of art which he has found the means of providing! The simple, but at the same time the great and wonderful contrivance by which has been produced the profusion of accommodations with which the civilized life of man abounds, is the division of labour. Wherever a society can be supposed to consist of one class of labourers only, the cultivators of the soil, it must be poor and wretched. Even if each individual, or each family, may be supposed so far to vary their labour as to provide themselves with some species of coarse garment, or some rude hut to shelter them from the weather, the affairs of the society must still be miserable. Let us next consider the simplest division of labour which we can well imagine. Let us suppose that the society becomes divided into husbandmen, and into the manufacturers merely of their agricultural tools, of their garments and houses. How much more completely would the community almost immediately, or at least as soon as the manufacturers acquired any dexterity in their trades, be provided with the accommoda-

tions which we have just enumerated? Their riches
would be augmented. The labour of the same
men would now yield a much larger produce. It
is to the manufacturers however, it is to that division of labour which set them apart as a distinct
class, that this superiority of produce, that this
augmentation of riches, is entirely owing.

'The greatest improvement,' says Dr. Smith,
'in the productive powers of labour, and the
'greater part of the skill, dexterity, and judg-
'ment, with which it is any where directed or
'applied, seem to have been the effects of the
'division of labor. ****. It is the great mul-
'tiplication of the productions of all the different
'arts, in consequence of the division of labour,
'which occasions in a well governed society that
'universal opulence, which extends itself to the
'lowest ranks of the people.' The effects indeed
of the division of labour, are surprising and almost miraculous. But as the division of labour
commenced with the first formation of a class of
manufacturers, and as it is in manufactures that
the division of labour has been carried to the
greatest height, the business of agriculture being
much less susceptible of this improvement, the
whole or the greater part of the opulence, which
is diffused in society by the division of labour, is
to be ascribed to manufactures. The same is the
case with machinery. How much the production
of commodities is accelerated and increased by
the invention and improvement of machines, requires no illustration. It is chiefly in manufactures, that this great advantage too has been

reaped. In agriculture, the use of machinery is much more limited.

Every view of the subject affords an argument against the intricate but flimsy reasonings of the *Economistes*. In the infancy of manufactures, when the distaff alone, and other simple and tedious instruments are known, let us suppose that a piece of cloth is prepared. Mr. Spence informs us, that nothing is added to the wealth of the society, by the preparation of this piece of cloth, because a quantity of corn equal to it in value, has during the preparation been consumed by the manufacturers. Let us suppose, however, that, suddenly, spinning and other machines are invented, by which the same labourers are enabled to prepare six similar pieces, in the same time, and while they are consuming the same quantity of corn. If their manufacture in the former case replaced the corn which they consumed; in this case it replaces it six times. Will Mr. Spence deny that in such instances manufactures are productive of wealth? But how many more than six times have the productive powers of labour in the arts and manufactures been multiplied since the first division and distribution of occupations?

Without any further accumulation of arguments, I may take it I believe for granted, that the insufficiency of Mr. Spence's reasonings, to prove that manufactures are not a source of wealth, sufficiently appears. Let us now therefore proceed to another of his topics.

CHAP V.

Commerce.

BY commerce, in the language of Mr. Spence's pamphlet, is meant trade with foreign nations; and we have no objection, on the present occasion at least, to follow his example. Mr. Spence begins his investigation of this subject with the following paragraph:

'As all commerce naturally divides itself into
'commerce of import and export, I shall in the
'first place, endeavour to prove, that no riches,
'no increase of national wealth, can in any case
'be derived from commerce of import; and, in
'the next place, that, although national wealth
'may, in some cases, be derived from commerce
'of export, yet, that Britain in consequence of
'particular circumstances, has not derived, nor
'does derive, from this branch of commerce, any
'portion of her national wealth; and, conse-
'quently, that her riches, her prosperity, and
'her power are intrinsic, derived from her own
'resources, independent of commerce, and might
'and will exist, even though her trade should be
'annihilated. These positions, untenable as at
'first glance they may seem, I do not fear being
'able to establish to the satisfaction of those, who
'will dismiss from their mind the deep rooted

* See pp. 38, 39.

' prejudices, with which, on this subject, they
' are warped; and who, no longer contented with
' examining the mere surface of things, shall de-
' termine to penetrate through every stratum of
' the mine which conceals the grand truths of
' political economy.'

Let us begin then with the most earnest endeavour, according to the recommendation of
Mr. Spence, to purge our minds from ' prejudices,' attending solely to the reasons in favor of
those positions, ' which seem untenable at first
glance.' Let us summon up courage to follow
his deep and adventurous example, and not contented with remaining ingloriously ' at the surface,' let us clap on the miner's jacket and
trowsers, and descend in the bucket with Mr.
Spence; that, as truth, according to the ancient
philosopher, lay at the bottom of a well, we may
find ' the grand truths of political economy,' at
the bottom of a coal pit.

As trade with foreign nations consists of two
distinct branches, commerce of import, and commerce of export, it will be convenient for us to
consider each of these divisions separately. This
circumstance will divide the present chapter into
two articles.

Article First, Commerce of Import.

The reason which Mr. Spence adduces to prove
to those, who dismiss their deep rooted prejudices, and penetrate into the mine of political
economy, that commerce of import can never

produce wealth, he states in the following terms;
' Every one must allow, that for whatever a na-
' tion purchases in a foreign market, it gives an
' adequate value, either in money or in other
' goods; so far then, certainly, it gains no profit
' nor addition to its wealth. It has changed one
sort of wealth for another, but it has not in-.
' creased the amount, it was before possessed of*.'

We have had already occasion to wonder at the
oversights or mistakes, which so acute a man as
Mr. Spence has committed, and we are here
again brought into the same predicament. Might
he not, without any great depth, without descend-
ing far below the ' surface,' have reflected that a
commodity may be of one value in one place, and
of another value in another place. A ton of
hemp for example, which in Russia is worth
£50, is in Great Britain worth £65. When we
have exported therefore a quantity of British
goods, which in Britain is worth £50, and have
imported in lieu of them a ton of hemp, which
is worth £65, the riches of he country are by
this exchange increased fifteen pounds†. We
might illustrate this observation by a variety of
examples. The meaning and force of it however
are already sufficiently apparent. Whenever a cargo

* Brit. Indepen. of Com. p. 39.

† For the sake of preserving the argument as simple as
possible, the consideration of freight and charges is not here
introduced, as this affects in no degree the reasoning, and only
requires that an abatement be made from the amount of profit.
It is not the quantity of profit, but profit in any quantity,
which the argument respects. The customary profit of trade
will always be made, as long as the business continues.

of goods of any sort is exported, and a cargo of other goods, bought with the proceeds of the former, is imported, whatever the goods imported exceed in value the goods exported, beyond the expence of importation, is so much clear gain to the country; and to this amount are the riches of the country increased by the transaction.

Mr. Spence, however, has an argument to shew, that this reasoning is inconclusive. He allows, that the merchant, by whom the goods have been imported, makes a profit to the above amount. But this he says is no gain to the country. The additional sum, which the merchant obtains for the goods imported, is derived from the British consumer. Whatever the one gains therefore the other loses, and the country is nothing the richer. It is curious that this argument would prove the country to be not a farthing the richer, if all the goods imported were got by the merchants for nothing, or were even created by a miracle in their warehouses. In this case too, whatever the merchants obtained for their miraculous goods, would be drawn from the British consumer, and whatever the one gained the other would lose; consequently the country would be not a pin the richer for this extraordinary augmentation of goods. The reader will probably conclude, that an argument of this sort proves too much. We may recollect too, that this is neither more nor less than the argument which Mr. Spence produced, to prove, that manufactures were productive of no wealth. Whatever the manufactured commodity brought, beyond the

value of the raw produce consumed in the manufacture, was drawn, he said, from the purchaser,
who lost whatever the seller gained. On this
account he concluded, that the country was not
the richer for manufactures. This argument we
found to be so weak, that it implied the mistake
of the sale of a commodity for its manufacture.
In the present case too, the confusion and misapprehension are nearly the same. The transfer
of the imported goods from one British subject to
another, is mistaken for the exchange of a quantity of goods between Great Britain and a foreign
country. The sale of the goods at home renders
not the country richer, it is the purchase of them
abroad, with a quantity of British goods of less
value.

What we have already said appears to be perfectly sufficient to expose the fallacy of Mr.
Spence's arguments to prove the inutility of
commerce of import*. We may add, however,
a few observations, to explain to the reader
somewhat more distinctly in what manner commerce of import does contribute to national
wealth. On the subject of political economy, it
seems best to recur as often as possible to parti-

* Mr. Spence's notions appear not to be very steady even
on this subject. Thus, he says, (p. 8.) speaking of the attempts to exclude our commerce, that, ' he has rather been
' inclined to pity the poor inhabitants of the countries, who
' are prevented from buying our manufactures, than us that
' are hindered from selling them.' Now, what he pities
those poor countries for, is, that they are not enabled to carry
on an import trade. Why? if import trade can never add
any thing to wealth!

cular instances; it being so very common for authors, who indulge, like Mr. Spence, in very general terms, to bewilder both themselves and their readers. We import iron for example from the Baltic, though in certain favourable situations, where coal and the ore are found in the same vicinity, we make it at home. How does it appear, that this importation is advantageous? For this reason, that in all other cases but those specified, we can buy it cheaper abroad, than we can make it at home. We send forth a hundred pounds worth of goods, and we purchase with those goods a quantity of iron, which is worth more than one hundred pounds. Whatever this superiority of value exceeds the charges of importation is gain to the country.

To render this observation still more applicable to Mr. Spence's principles, we may show how the instance resolves itself even into the rude produce of the soil. On making a ton of iron in Great Britain, let us suppose, that the labourers, &c. employed in providing the ore and the coals, and in smelting and preparing the metal, have consumed ten quarters of corn. Every ton of iron therefore prepared in Great Britain costs ten quarters of corn. Let us suppose, that in the preparation of a certain quantity of British manufactures, nine quarters of corn have been consumed; and let us suppose, that this quantity of goods will purchase in the Baltic a ton of iron, and afford, besides, the expence requisite for importing the iron into Britain. Is there not an evident saving of a quarter of corn, in the acquisition of this ton of iron? Is not the country one quarter of corn the richer, by means of its importation? In the importation of a thousand such tons, is it not a thousand quarters richer?

It is curious, that Mr. Spence, whether by chance or design, I know not, has chosen all his examples of importation among invidious instances. He always illustrates his arguments by the importation of luxuries, of articles of immediate consumption, as tea for example, which being speedily used, seem not to add to the stock of the country, or to form part of its riches. This, however, if it is intended to have any effect, is only an argument to the ignorance of his readers; for the nature of the case is in no respect different. Why should Mr. Spence object to the commerce in articles of immediate consumption, when the produce of the land itself consists chiefly of articles of immediate consumption? Is the land not a source of wealth, because its chief produce is corn, which is generally all consumed within less than eighteen months from the time of its production?

To make indeed any distinction in this argument between articles of necessity, and articles of luxury, is absolutely nugatory. Whenever a country advances a considerable way beyond the infancy of society, it is a small portion of the members of the community who are employed in providing the mere necessaries of life. By far the greater proportion of them are employed in providing supply to other wants of man. Now in this case, as well as in the former, the sole question is, whether a particular description of wants can be most cheaply supplied at home or abroad. If a certain number of manufacturers employed at home can, while they are consuming 100 quarters of corn, fabricate a quantity of goods, which goods will purchase abroad a portion of supply to some of the luxurious wants of the community which it would have required the consumption of 150 quarters at home to produce; in this case too the country is 50 quarters the richer for the importation. It has the same supply of luxuries for 50 quarters of corn less, than if that supply had been prepared at home.

The commerce of one country with another, is in fact merely an extension of that division of labour by which so many benefits are conferred upon the human race. As the same country is rendered the richer by the trade of one province with another; as its labour becomes thus infinitely more divided, and more productive than it could otherwise have been; and as the mutual supply to each other of all the accommodations which one province has and another wants, multiplies the accommodations of the whole, and the country becomes thus in a wonderful degree more opulent and happy; the same beautiful train of consequences is observable in the world at large, that great empire, of which the different kingdoms and tribes of men may be regarded as the provinces. In this magnificent empire too one province is favourable to the production of one species of accommodation and another province to another. by their mutual intercourse they are enabled to sort and to distribute their labour as most peculiarly suits the genius of each particular spot. The labour of the human race thus becomes much more productive, and every species of accommodation is afforded in much greater abundance. The same number of labourers whose efforts might have been expended in producing a very insignificant quantity of home-made luxuries, may thus in Great-Britain produce a quantity of articles for exportation, accommodated to the wants of other places, and peculiarly suited to the genius of Britain to furnish, which will purchase for her an accumulation of the luxuries of every quarter of the globe. There is not a greater proportion of her population employed in administering to her luxuries, in consequence of her commerce, there is probably a good deal less; but their labour is infinitely more productive; the portion of commodities which the people of Great-Britain acquire by means of the same labour, is vastly greater.

Article Second; Commerce of Export.

Mr. Spence's reasoning concerning commerce of export is rather more complicated than that concerning commerce of import. ' It is plain,' he says,* ' that in some cases an increase of nati-
' onal wealth may be drawn from commerce of ex-
' port. The value obtained in foreign markets
' for the manufactures which a nation exports,
' resolves itself into the value of the food which

* See his pamphlet, p. 43.

'has been expended in manufacturing them, and
'the profit of the master manufacturer and the
'exporting merchant. These profits are undoubt-
'edly national profit. Thus, when a lace-manu-
'facturer has been so long employed in the manu-
'facturing a pound of flax into lace, that his
'subsistence during that period has cost £30;
'this sum is the real worth of the lace; and if it
'be sold at home, whether for £30 or £60, the
'nation is, as has been shewn, no richer for this
'manufacture. But if this lace be exported to
'another country, and there sold for £60, it is
'undeniable that the exporting nation has added
'£30 to its wealth by its sale, since the cost to it
'was only £30.' Allowing, however, that this
advantage, without any abatement, was drawn by
Great-Britain from her export commerce, its utmost amount, he says, would still be trifling, and
our exaggerated notions of the value of our trade,
ridiculous. ' Great-Britain,' he informs us,* ' in
'the most prosperous years of her commerce, has
'exported to the amount of about fifty millions
'sterling. If we estimate the profit of the master
'manufacturer, and the exporting merchant, at
'20 per cent. on this, it will probably be not far
'from the truth; certainly it will be fully as much
'as in these times of competition is likely to be
'gained. Great-Britain then gains annually by
'her commerce of export ten millions.' This
sum, he tells us, is a mere trifle in the amount of
our annual produce. ' More than *twice* this sum,

* See his pamphlet, p. 43.

he says,* ‘ is paid for the interest of the national
‘ debt! More than *four times* this sum is paid to
‘ the government in taxes!’† This sum, however,
insufficient as it is to justify our lofty conceptions
of the value of our commerce, is in reality, he at
last assures us, not gained by Great-Britain.
The reason which he brings in proof of this assertion, is the point to the examination of which we
now proceed.

Great-Britain, he says, and in proof of this he
enters into a long dissertation, imports regularly
to as great an amount as she exports, and for that
reason she gains nothing by her export trade.
But how then? What else would Mr. Spence have

---

* See his pamphlet, p. 44.

† Mr. Spence is but an indifferent political arithmetician.
He computes the gains upon the fifty millions of British exports, by allowing twenty per cent. for the profits of the
master manufacturer and the exporting merchant, at ten millions a year. But from this sum, says he, (p. 44) ‘ we ought
‘ certainly to deduct the annual amount of our commercial
‘ losses at sea. The greater part of our exports, as well as
‘ of our imports, being insured by British underwriters, the
‘ whole amount which they annually pay is so much dead loss
‘ to the nation deducting the premiums which they receive
‘ from foreign countries.’ He here makes the poor nation
sustain its losses at sea twice over. The premiums of insurance
paid by the merchants to the underwriters cover the whole of
the losses with a profit. These premiums are as little charged
by the merchant to his account of profit as the expence of
freight. His profits are reckoned with a complete deduction
of those premiums; and when we say that his profit is ten
per cent. or twenty per cent. full account is made of loss.
To make us first deduct our losses from the profits of the merchant, and then make a deduction of them again, for the
sums paid by the underwriters, is hard dealing.

us to do? Would he have us export our goods for nothing? And is that the plan which he would propose to make the country gain by her commerce? Ought we to carry our commodities to foreigners, and beg them only to accept of the articles; but above all things not to insist upon making us take any thing in payment; as this would be the certain way to prevent us from gaining by the trade?

For what on the other hand is it that Mr. Spence would recommend to us to get for our goods? If we receive not other goods, the only return we can receive seems to be money. Would Mr. Spence then tell us that we should get rich by receiving every year gold and silver for our fifty millions of exports? Not to insist upon the inherent absurdity of such a notion, let us only observe how inconsistent it would be with his own declared opinions? He warned us, in a passage already quoted,* against conceiving that wealth consists in gold and silver merely. He assured us that †' Spain has plenty of gold and silver, yet she ' has no wealth, whilst Britain is wealthy with ' scarcely a guinea.' He informs us farther,‡ ' that a nation which has abundance of gold and ' silver, is in fact not richer than if it had none. ' It has paid an equal value of some other wealth ' for them, and there is no good reason why it ' should be desirous of having this rather than

---

* See p. 18 of this pamphlet. † Ibid.
‡ See p. 18 of Mr. Spence's pamphlet, ' Britain Independent of Commerce.'

'any other species of wealth; for the only supe-
'riority in value which the precious metals possess
'over other products of the labour of man, is
'their fitness for being the instruments of circu-
'lation and exchange. But in this point of view
'the necessity of having gold and silver no longer
'exists; experience has in modern times evinced
'that paper, or the promissory notes of men of
'undoubted property, form a circulating medium
'fully as useful and much less expensive.'

He here informs us expressly that gold and silver are in no respect more to be desired than any
other imported commodity. But the importing
of other commodities he assured us was the cause
which prevented our commerce of export from
being a source of wealth. We now see that by
his own confession gold and silver are in the same
predicament with other imported commodities.
But, if in order to gain by our commerce of export, we must receive in return neither goods nor
money, we see no alternative that is left, except,
as we said before, giving our goods away for
nothing.

It may serve to render the subject still more
clear, if I add a few words in the farther explanation of money. The true idea of money is
neither more nor less than that of a commodity
which is bought and sold like other commodities.
In dealings with foreign nations, that class of
transactions which we are now considering, this
will very easily appear. When British goods, sold
abroad, are paid for in money, it is not the deno-
mination of the foreign coin which the merchant

regards, it is the quantity of gold and silver which it contains. It is its value as bullion merely that he estimates in the exchange; and it is in the form of bullion, not of foreign coin, that the gold and silver, when it is in gold and silver that he receives his payment, is imported. The importation of gold and silver, therefore, differs in no respect from the importation of platinum, zinc, copper, or any other metal. A certain part of it being taken occasionally to be stamped as money, makes not an atom of difference between the cases. It appears, therefore, with additional evidence, that if the importation of other commodities in exchange for the British goods which we export, annihilates the advantage of the exportation; so likewise does the importation of gold and silver. Again, therefore, we ask in what possible way are we to derive wealth from our commerce of export, but by the generous disposal of our goods for nothing to the kind and friendly nations who will please to receive them.

If we trace this subject a little farther, we shall perceive how the importation of money would disorder the policy of Mr. Spence. It is very evident that the gold and silver which can be of any use in a nation, does not exceed a certain quantity. In Great-Britain, where it is almost banished from the medium of exchange, the annual supply which is wanted, cannot be very large. To render what we receive, above this trifling supply, of any utility, it must again travel abroad to purchase something for which we may have occasion. But in this case again it administers to the traffic of importation; and thus, by the very act of its becoming useful, produces the effect which Mr. Spence says cuts off the advantage to be derived from commerce of export.

We have yet, however, to examine an important resource of Mr. Spence's theory. He makes a distinction between commodities, which are of a durable, and commodities which are of a perishable nature. The commodities he says, which are of a durable nature, are much more valuable as articles of wealth, than articles which are of a perishable nature; and the country which produces or purchases the one, contributes much more to the augmentation of its wealth, than the country which acquires the latter. It sometimes happens to more accurate reasoners than Mr. Spence, that one part of their theory clashes with another. But we think it does not very often happen, that a man of Mr. Spence's powers of mind, (for it is rather in the want of practice in speculation, than in want of capacity for it, that his defect seems to lie) so obviously becomes the antagonist of his own doctrine. In the whole train of commodities, are any of a more perishable nature than all the most important productions of the land? Of many of the manufactures, on the other hand, the productions are of a very durable sort, as the manufactures for example of tooth-picks, and of glass beads for the ladies. According to this ingenious distinction, therefore, could we increase the manufacture of tooth-picks, and glass beads, by diminishing the production of corn, we should contribute to the riches of the country.

The use which Mr. Spence makes of this distinction, is notable. The greater part of the articles of British importation, he says, are of a perishable nature; whereas her articles of exportation are of a durable nature; for this reason she ought to be considered as losing by her foreign trade. 'We do,' says he*, ' gain annually a ' few millions by our export trade, and if we re- ' ceived these profits in the precious metals, or ' even in durable articles of wealth, we might ' be said to increase our riches by commerce; ' but we spend at least twice the amount of what ' we gain, in luxuries, which deserve the name ' of wealth but for an instant, which are here to ' day, and to morrow are annihilated. How then ' can our wealth be augmented by such a trade?'

We may here remark another instance, in which the ideas of Mr. Spence wage hostilities with one another. We shall hereafter find, that he recommends consumption and luxury, as favorable to the prosperity of the state. Yet here we perceive, that all his reasons against the utility of commerce, terminate in a quarrel with the importation of articles of luxury †.

---

* See his pamphlet, p. 53.

† Mr. Spence is very apt to shift the ground of his arguments. He began his dissertation on the inutility of our export commerce, p. 47, thus; ' I grant, that when a nation ' exports considerably more than she imports, the profits ' charged on her exported goods, will be national profits; but,

Nothing was ever more unfortunate than this distinction of Mr. Spence. We have seen before, in the article on commerce of import, that no distinction in the question of wealth exists between the commerce in articles of luxury, and any other. Whatever arguments therefore are drawn from this distinction, are addressed to the ignorance of those, who, as Mr. Spence says, ' skim the surface.' The only distinction of importance, which can be made between one sort of commodities and another, is that between the commodities which are destined to serve for immediate and unproductive consumption, and the commodities which are destined to operate as the instruments or means of production. Of the first sort, are all articles of luxury; and even the necessaries of life of all those, who are not employed in productive labour. Of the latter sort, are the materials of our manufactures, as wool, iron, cotton, &c., whatever forms the machinery and tools of productive labour, and even the

' inasmuch as *Britain imports as much as she exports*, and in-
' asmuch as *a great proportion of her imports consists of luxu-*
' *ries, which are speedily consumed;* from *these* circumstances I
' contend, that her wealth derives no augmentation from her
' commerce of export.' We see, that his reasons against the utility of commerce in this passage, are two; 1st, The equality of our imports with our exports, of whatever sort these imports may be; 2d, The perishable nature of a great part of these imports. In the passage just quoted in the text, we perceive that Mr. Spence gives up the first of these reasons, allowing, that if we imported durable articles, we might gain by commerce, and insists only upon the last. We lose by our commerce, he says here, only because we import articles of a perishable nature,

food and clothes of the labourer. Of the commodities which administer to productive labour, it is evidently absurd to make any distinction between those which are durable, and those, which, to use a phrase of Mr. Spence, are, ' evanescent ;' as the most evanescent of them all has performed its part, before it vanishes, and replaced itself with a profit. Thus, the drugs of the dyer, even the coals which are consumed in his furnace, the corn which feeds his workmen, or the milk, one of the most perishable of all commodities, which they may use in their diet, have performed their part as completely, and to the amount of their value as usefully as the iron lever, with which he drives his press. On the other hand, when articles are destined for immediate and unproductive consumption, it seems a consideration of very trifling importance, whether they are articles which are likely to be all used in the course of one year, or in the course of several years. When a rouge for the ladies cheeks, which may be kept for any time, and hoarded up to any quantity, is imported, we surely cannot regard the interests of the country as much more consulted, than when the most evanescent luxury which Mr. Spence can conceive is introduced into it. When it is on a distinction without a difference, that Mr. Spence's argument against commerce ultimately depends, his doctrine must rest on a sandy foundation*.

* How often, and how justly has it been observed, that the costly palaces, and other luxuries of the greatest durability, on which Louis the XIVth expended vast sums of

Mr. Spence's opinions, however, on this subject are very wonderful. ' Of two nations,' he says*, ' if one employed a part of its population
' in manufacturing articles of hardware, another
' in manufacturing wine, both destined for home
' consumption; though the nominal value of both
' products should be the same, and the hardware
' should be sold in one country for £10,000,
' and the wine in the other for the same sum, yet
' it is evident, that the wealth of the two countries
' would, in the course of a few years, be very
' different. If this system were continued for
' five years, in the one country, the manufacturers
' of hardware would have drawn from the con-
' sumers of this article, £50,000 ; and, at the
' same time, this manufacture being of so un-
' perishable a nature, the purchasers of it would
' still have in existence the greater part of the
' wealth they had bought; whereas, in the other
' nation, though the wine manufacturers would
' have also drawn to themselves £50,000 from
' the consumers of wine, yet these last would have
' no vestige remaining of the luxury they had
' consumed. It is evident, therefore, that at the

money, contributed as certainly to the exhaustion and impoverishment of France, as the expensive wars which he carried on, or the daily extravagance of his prodigal court? Mr. Spence will surely allow that the pyramids of Egypt are sufficiently durable. Yet the political philosopher would amuse us, who should advise us to enrich our country, by building a few of these durable structures. Durability then is not the philosopher's stone ; one thing may be more useful in half an hour, than another thing in twenty years.

* See his pamphlet, p. 51.

' end of five years, the wealth of the former
' nation would be much greater than that of the
' latter, though both had annually brought into
' existence wealth to an equal nominal amount.'

Now what is the idea which seems to be in-
volved in this explanation ? It is, that the nation
which imports articles of a durable nature grows
rich by hoarding them up.   It is curious, that the
very idea, and in fact the very example, which Dr.
Smith brings forward as so absurd that it might
serve to cover with ridicule the mercantile system, is actually adduced by Mr. Spence, in the
simplicity of his heart, as a solid reason to prove
the inutility of commerce. Dr. Smith thus remarks : ' Consumable commodities, it is said, are
' soon destroyed ; whereas gold and silver are of a
' more durable nature, and were it not for their
' continual exportation, might be accumulated
' for ages together, to the incredible augmenta-
' tion of the real wealth of the country.   Nothing,
' therefore, it is pretended, can be more disad-
' vantageous to any country, than the trade
' which consists in the exchange of such lasting
' for such perishable commodities.   We do not,
' however, reckon that trade disadvantageous
' which consists in the exchange of the hardware
' of England for the wines of France ; and yet
' hardware is a very durable commodity, and were
' it not for this continual exportation, might too
' be accumulated for ages together, to the incre-
' dible augmentation of the pots and pans of the
' country.   But it readily occurs that the number
' of such utensils is in every country necessarily li-

1

' mited by the use which there is for them;
' that it would be absurd to have more pots and
' pans than were necessary for cooking the
' victuals usually consumed there; and that, if the
' quantity of victuals was to increase, the number
' of pots and pans would readily increase along
' with it, a part of the increased quantity of the
' victuals being employed in purchasing them, or
' in maintaining an additional number of work-
' men, whose business it was to make them.'

In fact nothing can well be more weak than
to consider the augmentation of national riches,
by the accumulation of durable articles of luxury,
as a consideration of moment. The value of the
whole amount of them in any country is never
considerable, and it is evident that whatever they
cost is as completely withdrawn from maintaining
productive industry, as that which is paid for the
most perishable articles.* Mr. Spence has an
extremely indistinct and wavering notion of national wealth. He seems on the present occasion
to regard it as consisting in the actual accumulation of the money and goods which at any time
exists in the nation. But this is a most imperfect
and erroneous conception. The wealth of a country consists in her powers of annual production,
not in the mere collection of articles which may

---

* When Mr. Spence sets so great a value upon articles of
durability, he ought to recollect his own doctrine (see p 16
of Mr. Spence's pamphlet) ' that the manufacturer transmutes
' wealth of so perishable a nature as food into the more dura-
' ble wealth manufactures.' Must he not then, according to
the doctrine of durability, augment the national wealth ?

at any instant of time be fonnd in existence.
How inadequate an idea would he have of the
wealth of Great Britain who should fix his ideas
merely upon the goods in the warehouses of her
merchants, and upon the accommodations in the
houses of individuals; and should not rather direct
his attention to the prodigious amount of goods
and accommodations which is called into existence annually by the miraculous powers of our
industry? The only part, it is evident, of the
existing collection of commodities which in any
degree contributes to augment the annual produce, the permanent riches of the country, is
that part which administers to productive labour ;
the machines, tools, and raw materials which are
employed in the different species of manufacturing
and agricultural industry. All other articles whether durable or perishable are lost to the annual
produce, and the smaller the quantity of either so
much the better.

To trace however these ideas as far as Mr.
Spence pleases ; let us suppose that our merchants
instead of importing perfumes, for example, for
the nose, should import ornaments for the hair
and other similar trinkets of the greatest durability. When or how can these be supposed to
be of any utility or value ? The use of them, it
is evident, is as frivolous and as little conducive
to any valuable end as that of the perfumes. It is
only in the idea of their sale therefore that they
can be considered as more valuable than the perfumes. They might still be sold for something
after the perfumes are consumed. In the first

place, the sale of half worn trinkets or hardware would not, it is likely, be very productive. But observe the nature of the sale itself. What a nation sells, it sells to some other nation. Should it then sell its accumulation of trinkets and hardware, it must import something in lieu of them. This must be either perishable articles, or such durable articles as the hardware which was exported; for money, even according to Mr. Spence, forms no distinction. But this fresh cargo of durable articles is in the same predicament with the former; useless while it remains, and only capable of augmenting the riches of the country when it is resold. But this course it is evident may be repeated to infinity, and still the augmentation of wealth be as little attained as before. It is seldom that a false argument in political economy admits of so complete a reduction to absurdity as this.

We have thus with some minuteness examined the validity of what Mr. Spence brings, in the shape of argument, to prove that the export commerce of Great Britain is productive of no wealth.* A very short and conclusive argument however was sufficient for the refutation of this boasted

---

* Great Britain is understood by the world to gain more by commerce than all other nations put together. According to Mr. Spence, she is in the singular situation of losing by it, while all other nations gain. He told us already (see p. 35), that he pitied those nations from which Bonaparte excluded our goods. He tells us again (Brit. Independent of Com. p. 56) 'We shall find, that it is Europe, Asia, America,— 'all the countries with which she trades,—not Britain, that is 'enriched by her commerce.' Commerce then may enrich; it is only Great Britain that is silly enough to mismanage it!

doctrine. The imports of Great Britain are equal, he says, in amount to her exports, and they are chiefly of a perishable nature. What Great Britain therefore might gain by her exports she loses by her imports. But we have already proved, in the preceding article, that commerce of import is itself a source of gain, and that, whether the articles imported are of a perishable or a durable nature. Whatever therefore is gained by our commerce of export is so far from being diminished by our commerce of import, that this last affords a gain equal in amount to that of the former. The profits of commerce are doubled by the operation of import.*

There is another view of this subject exhibited by Mr. Spence, which it may yet be of some importance to consider. Though the grand axiom of the *Economistes*, that the only source of wealth is land, is undoubtedly, he says, founded in truth, yet an application which they make of this axiom to the present affairs of Europe is erroneous. Though it is † ‘ the natural order of prosperity

When it suits Mr. Spence’s purpose he can represent commerce as a very powerful agent in national prosperity. Thus he says (Brit. Indep. of Com. p. 84) “ Should the blacks ‘ of St. Domingo be able to resist the attempts of the French ‘ for their subjection, and succeed in establishing a regular ‘ independent government, they will not fail, *by means of* ‘ *their commercial intercourse,* speedily to become civilized and ‘ powerful.’ Mr. Spence generally admits the effect of commerce in promoting civilization; but how can it render a nation *powerful,* but by rendering it opulent ?

† See p. 20 of his pamphlet, Brit. Indep. of Commerce.

' in a state that agriculture produces manufac-
' tures, not manufactures agriculture; yet the
' case seems very different with Europe, and an
' attention to facts will prove, *that in Britain agri-*
' *culture has thriven only in consequence of the in-*
' *fluence of manufactures ; and that the increase of*
' *this influence is requisite to its farther extension.*'
It is needless to state the proof which he adduces
of these positions; for it is neither more nor
less than a repetition, in Mr. Spence's own manner, of the view which Dr. Smith exhibits* of
the progress of industry in the feudal governments
of modern Europe; where the slow and impercep-
tible insinuation of commerce burst asunder the
bands of feudal tyranny, and instead of the sloth
and poverty of servitude introduced the industry
and opulence of liberty. It is enough for us at
present to advert attentively to the positions which
Mr. Spence here so emphatically announces, that
such have been, and such are, the actual circumstances of Europe, that agriculture neither could
have thriven, nor can yet thrive, but by means of
manufactures. On this single admission, me-
thinks, one might conclude that it was rather a
rash doctrine to promulgate that commerce is of
no utility to Great Britain, and that she might
contemplate the loss of it with little emotion.

But having seen that manufactures, by Mr.
Spence's own admission, are absolutely necessary
to the prosperity of Europe in her present circum-

* See Wealth of Nations, B. III. particularly the last three
chapters.

stances, particularly in the present arrangement
of her landed property; let us next see what is
that state of things to which alone he admits that
his doctrine respecting land and commerce is applicable. Having shewn that the conclusion
which the *Economistes* drew, and drew very logically, from their principles, that till the whole
land of every country be cultivated in the most
complete manner, manufactures should receive
little encouragement, will not apply to the circumstances of modern Europe, he next proceeds
to describe that state of affairs to which the principles and conclusions of that sect do apply. Observe then what is that arrangement of the
circumstances of Europe, what the changes
from their present situation, which are requisite
to adopt them for the practical operation of the
doctrines of the *Economistes.* ‘If the question
‘ were,’ says Mr. Spence,* ‘ on what system may
‘ the greatest prosperity be enjoyed by the bulk of
‘ society, there can be no doubt that the system
‘ recommended by the Economistes, which directs
‘ the attention of every member of society to be
‘ turned to agriculture, would be most effectual to
‘ this end. But such a system could be effica-
‘ ciously established in Europe in no other way
‘ than by the overthrow of all the present laws of
‘ property, and by a revolution which would be as
‘ disasterous in its ultimate consequences as it
‘ would be unjust and impracticable in its institu-
‘ tion. *This system could be acted upon only by*

* See his Pamphlet, p. 27.

' *the passing an Agrarian law* ; *by the division of*
' *the whole soil of a country in equal portions*
' *amongst its inhabitants.*'—Let us here intreat
Mr. Spence to pause for a moment, and to reflect
upon the practical lessons which he is so eager
to teach us. The present course of industry by
manufactures and commerce he admits is adapted
to the present circumstances of Europe, and
that all the prosperity which she exhibits is
owing to it ; the application of the doctrine that
all prosperity is owing to agriculture would require, he says, ' the division of the whole soil
' of the country in equal portions amongst its
' inhabitants, a revolution which would be as
' disasterous in its ultimate consequences, as it
' would be unjust and impracticable in its insti-
' tution ;' yet on the strength of this system he
would have us believe that commerce is of no
utility ; he would have us conduct our affairs on
a plan which is not applicable to the present situation of the world, and abandon the course by
which we have attained our actual prosperity.*

Another admission here of Mr. Spence is truly

* It is truly amusing to compare some of the parts of Mr.
Spence's pamphlet with other parts. He here tells us that the
most prosperous condition of society, would be that established
on the principles of the *Economistes*, which require the greatest subdivision of landed property. Yet hear him on the subject of a great subdivision of landed property, in another passage ; (note p. 45) ' In France, where there is an infinity of
' small estates of ten and twenty, and even so low as two and
' three acres each, *which are the bane of all national increase of*
' *wealth*, probably more than half the population is employed
' in agriculture.'

pleasant. An equal division of the land, he says, would be an institution *impracticable*; and well indeed is the observation founded. How could mankind ever agree about what is equal? Equal surfaces are very unequal in value; and the value is a circumstance so ambiguous and disputable, that it can never be accurately ascertained. Besides, the value of land is perpetually changing. In the hands of the industrious man it improves; in the hands of the slothful man it becomes barren. What then? In order to preserve our equality, must we take part of his improved land from the industrious man to give to the slothful? This would be giving a premium to sloth, and laying a tax, sufficient to operate as a prohibition, upon industry. We should thus have all our people slothful, and all our land barren. But independent of this, the number of people does not always remain the same. It is perpetually changing. That no one then might be without a share, it would be requisite to be making perpetual changes in the apportionment of the land; and thus no one would ever know what was or was not his land. He could never therefore expend any pains in the culture of it. With great justice then has Mr. Spence asserted that the institution of an Agrarian law is impracticable. Observe, however, another assertion of his: ‘ that the system of the ‘ Economistes can be efficaciously established, that ‘ it can be acted upon, in no other way than by an ‘ equal division of the soil.’ The system of the Economistes, then, cannot be established, but in an impossible state of things. It is a system not applicable to human affairs. It is therefore an absurdity.*

* There is one pretty important subject on which Mr. Spence has wonderfully changed his language, at least during the period between the publication of the second and third editions of his pamphlet. In his second edition, (p. 57,) he expressed himself on the famous question respecting *the balance of trade*, in the following manner; 'Ever since the 'publication of Dr. Adam Smith's Wealth of Nations, it has 'been usual for those who have embraced the Doctor's opi-'nions, to ridicule the axiom of the older politicians, viz. 'that for a nation to gain wealth by commerce, it is necessary 'it should export more than it imports, and receive the balance 'of trade in the precious metals. From what has been ob-'served, it will be obvious, that the absurdity charged by him 'and his followers on the doctrine of the Pettys, the Davenants, 'and the Deckers, of former times, is by no means so convin-'cingly made out as they would have us to believe. It ap-'pears these ancient politicians had an accurate idea of the 'true nature of commerce, though they erred in attaching too 'much importance to it. They rightly considered commerce 'to be, as its derivation implies, an exchange of one commo-'dity for another ; and hence they justly conceived, that if a 'nation imported, in return for its exports, a quantity of com-'modities only equal in value to them, it would never get 'wealth by such an interchange of one value for another. 'The absurdity, then, charged upon this doctrine of the ba-'lance of trade, does not belong to the principle itself, which 'is founded in truth, but to its application.' This passage, so decidedly asserting the truth of the doctrine respecting the balance of trade, is entirely omitted in the third edition ; and instead of it, we find inserted, in a different place, the following passage ; ' Before I proceed,' (see 3d edit. p. 53) 'to advance the reasoning, and to point out the facts upon 'which this opinion is founded, it is necessary to shew, by a 'slight examination, the fallacy of the doctrine of the *balance* 'of trade; or the opinion that Britain accumulates riches from 'her commerce, by receiving every year a balance in the pre-'cious metals, in consequence of a constant excess of her ex-

It is perhaps not less remarkable that Mr. Spence himself proceeds, apparently unconscious that it is a refutation of his own doctrine which he is penning, to exhibit a proof that his system, even if it were capable of being introduced, could lead to no happiness; far from it ; but to a state of the greatest misery. ' Let us attend,' he says,* ' a moment to the results which would ensue from ' the establishment of such a system. If the ' twelve millions of inhabitants of Great-Britain ' were to have the seventy-three millions of acres ' of land, which this island is said to contain, di- ' vided amongst them, each individual receiving six ' acres as his share, there can be no doubt, that the ' condition of the great bulk of the people would ' be materially improved. Such a quantity of land ' would suffice for the production of meat, ' clothes and fire, of every thing necessary for ' comfortable existence ; and the peasant, no ' longer anxious about the means of providing ' bread for his family, might devote his abundant

' ports over her imports. Glaringly absurd as is this doctrine ' in the eyes of every tyro in political economy, and clearly as ' it has been demonstrated that no such balance can be received; ' we still, as a century ago, hear not only our newspaper poli- ' ticians, but our statesmen even, estimating the value of a ' branch of commerce by a reference to this exploded theory.' Does Mr. Spence abide by his own sentence, that he was more ignorant than a tyro in political economy, when his second edition was published ? Or will he exert his ingenuity to prove that his former passage was consistent with the present? If he can undertake this, I would not have advised him to expunge the former passage.

* Britain Indepen. of Commerce, p. 27.

' leisure to the cultivation of his mind, and thus
' realize, for a while, the golden dreams of a
' Condorcet or a Godwin. Yet however great
' the prosperity of such a state of society, it
' would be impossible for it to accumulate wealth.
' For, as all its members would provide their own
' food, there could be no sale for any surplus pro-
' duce, consequently no greater quantity would be
' raised than could be consumed, and at the end
' of the year, however great might have been the
' amount of the wealth brought into existence
' during that period by agriculture, not a trace of
' its existence would remain. Nor would the
' prosperity of such a state of society be of long
' duration. In a nation where such plenty reign-
' ed, the great command of the Creator, to in-
' crease and multiply, would act in full force, and
' the population would double in twenty-five
' years. Supposing then this state of things to
' continue, in seventy-five years from its establish-
' ment, Britain would contain ninety-six millions
' of souls, a number full as great as could possibly
' exist on seventy-three millions of acres of land.
' Here, then, misery would commence ; the diffi-
' culty of procuring subsistence would be greater
' to the whole of society than it now is to a small
' proportion ; population would be at a stand ;
' and on any occasional failure of food, all the
' dreadful consequences would ensue which so fre-
' quently befal the overpeopled country of China.'*

* It is remarkable in what obvious instances the unsteadi-
ness of Mr. Spence's ideas sometimes exhibits itself. Thus he
tells us, (p. 18 of his pamphlet) that ' gold and silver are un-

Scarcely could we desire an author to administer with more naïveté than this to his own confutation.

The doctrine of Mr. Spence then comes to this. If he admits absolutely the axiom of the *Economistes*, that land is the only source of wealth; then he must admit the whole of their system, which is built upon this axiom with logical and unquestionable exactness; but which we have found to be utterly impracticable in human affairs, and tending, even if it could be introduced, not to a state of happiness, but to a state of misery. Mr. Spence indeed asserts, over and over, that the axiom of the *Economistes* is an undoubted truth. Nay he enters into a chain of reasoning, or illustration, to prove that it is incontrovertible. We might therefore, by all the laws of reasoning, hold him to the conclusions which necessarily flow from it. But as he seems to wish to relax a little from the severity of the economical system, when he admits that it is inapplicable to the present circumstances of Europe, let us examine this amended doctrine. We shall find that no argu-

---

' doubtedly wealth.' Yet in the very same page he says, ' If gold and silver be but the *representative* of wealth and ' paper-money, the shadow of a shade,' &c. and then proceeds to found an important inference upon this assumption. In the next page, too, he says, ' Thus, then, whatever is the ' circulating medium, whether it be gold and silver, or paper, ' or both, *being but the representative of wealth*, there can be ' no difference as to the sources of wealth, between a nation ' which has, and one which has not, a circulating medium.' Mr. Spence, though evidently a man of education, has certainly been little accustomed to the business of accurate composition. We find, here, even a grammatical blunder.

ment can be founded upon it, which does not in reality give up the question. If Mr. Spence say that land is indeed the only source of wealth, but commerce, in the circumstances of modern Europe, is necessary to render the land productive, we may answer that all possible circumstances, even according to his own admission, will in the same manner require commerce, with the sole exception of that equal division of the land which is requisite to the establishment of the economical system. Commerce, therefore, is conducive to the prosperity of national affairs in every concurrence of circumstances consistent with the laws of human nature. If Mr. Spence still insist that commerce is only *mediately*, that land alone is *immediately*, the source of wealth, we shall certainly not dispute with him about a word, however incorrect we may deem the word which he employs: for in a question about the utility of food to the human body, we should not think it necessary very anxiously to contend with any newfangled physiologist who should argue that food does not contribute to the renovation and expansion of the bodily parts *immediately*, by direct conjunction, but only *mediately*, by stimulating the organs to accomplish this renovation and expansion. We should think it fully sufficient for the proof of our position, that food is useful, if it were admitted, that without food, such effects could not be produced. We should not, however, pay much attention to our physiological Instructor, should he proceed to his practical deductions, and tell us, ' Bonaparte will speedily be able to

' cut off your whole supplies of food; but be not
' in the least degree alarmed; only listen to me,
' and I will prove to you that food is not *immedi-*
' *ately*, but *mediately* useful to your bodies; there-
' fore you can do as well, or perhaps better,
' without it."*

---

* In one or two passages, particularly one inserted for the
first time in his 3d edition, Mr. Spence appears desirous to in-
sinuate that there is a distinction between manufactures for
home consumption, and manufactures for exports, in respect
to the encouragement of agriculture; as if manufactures for
home consumption contributed to the progress of agriculture,
but manufactures for exportation did not. It would have been
highly satisfactory, if this indeed be his opinion, for even that
does not certainly appear, had he but taken the trouble to give
us his reasons. As for me, I frankly own, I cannot so much
as conceive what those reasons could have been. I can recollect, however, very distinctly where Mr. Spence informs us
that manufactures for home consumption can never add to the
wealth of any country, but that manufactures for exportation
sometimes may. He tells us, p. 17, that his arguments ' have
' convincingly shewn that all wealth is created by agriculture,
' *none* by manufactures,' meaning manufactures for home consumption. He tells us too, p. 43, ' when a lace manufac-
' turer has been so long employed in the manufacturing a
' pound of flax into lace, that his subsistence during that pe-
' riod has cost £30, this sum is the real worth of the lace;
' and if it be sold *at home*, whether for £30 or £60, the na-
' tion *is no richer for this manufacture*. Bnt if this lace be ex-
' ported to another country, and there sold for £60, it is un-
' deniable that the exporting nation has added £30 to its
' wealth by its sale.' He says too, p. 57, 2d edition,
' However enlarged all the views, and however correct the
' reasoning of Dr. Smith, on most branches of the subject on
' which he wrote, he has in many instances fallen into errors,
' to the full as egregious as those which he condemns.' Let us
next hear the instances which he specifies; ' witness his doc-
"trine, that wealth is really created by manufactures made and

CHAP. VI.

Consumption.

THE doctrine of Mr. Spence respecting consumption is not less worthy of examination than his doctrine concerning production.

This author divides the members of a civilized society into four classes; the class of landowners—The class of cultivators—The class of manufacturers—And the unproductive class. ' As ' the whole revenue of a country,' he says,* ' is ' derived from its land; and as the class of land-' proprietors are the recipients of this revenue, it ' is evident that from this class must be drawn the ' revenues of the two other classes of society; ' the manufacturing and unproductive class. It ' is a condition, then, essential,' he adds, ' to the ' creation of national wealth, that the class of ' land-proprietors expend the greater part of the ' revenue which they derive from the soil. So ' long as they perform this duty, every thing goes ' on in its proper train. With the funds which ' the manufacturing and the unproductive classes ' appropriate to themselves from the expenditure ' of the class of landowners, they are enabled to ' purchase the food which the farmer offers to

' consumed at home; and his confused and unintelligible at-' tempt to confute the opposite tenets of the French Econo-' mists.' Ibid.

* See Mr. S's pamphlet, from p. 29 to 37.

F

‘ them. The farmer being enabled to dispose of
‘ his produce, acquires the funds necessary for the
‘ payment of his rent, &c. Let us make the
‘ supposition that fifty of our great landowners,
‘ each deriving twenty thousand pounds a year
‘ from his estates, which they have been accus-
‘ tomed to spend, were to be convinced by the ar-
‘ guments of Dr. Smith, that the practice of par-
‘ simony is the most effectual way of accumulating
‘ national riches, and should save the £1000000
‘ which their revenue amounted to. Is it not self-
‘ evident that the members of the manufacturing
‘ and unproductive classes, who had been accus-
‘ tomed to receive this sum, would have their power
‘ of consuming diminished? The farmer conse-
‘ quently could not sell so much of his produce,
‘ nor at so good a price as before. It is clear then
‘ that expenditure, not parsimony, is the pro-
‘ vince of the class of land proprietors; and that
‘ it is upon the due performance of this duty by
‘ the class in question, that the production of na-
‘ tional wealth depends. And not only does the
‘ production of national wealth depend upon the
‘ expenditure of the class of land-proprietors, but
‘ for the due increase of this wealth, and for the
‘ constantly progressive maintenance of the pros-
‘ perity of the community, it is absolutely requi-
‘ site that this class should go on progressively in-
‘ creasing its expenditure. It will follow, as a
‘ consequence, that in countries constituted as
‘ this and those composing the rest of Europe
‘ are, the increase of *luxury* is absolutely essential
‘ to their necessities. It is impossible exactly to

' define what are luxuries and what necessaries;
' yet a slight consideration will shew that a very
' great proportion of our manufactures cannot be
' included under the latter title. Every one knows
' that a few hundreds a year are sufficient to pro-
' cure all the necessaries and comforts of life : in
' what then can the sums above this amount,
' which are spent by the numbers in this country
' who have their £10,000 and £20,000 a year,
' be expended, but in luxuries ? And as from this
' consideration it is plain that the population of the
' manufacturing class, at present occupied in pro-
' viding necessaries, is fully equal to fabricate all
' that are wanted of this description, it follows
' that the additional population of this class can
' only be employed in the manufacture of new
' luxuries.'

This is the first part of our author's doctrine
concerning consumption, and I have been anxious
to exhibit a full view of it. Its nature and value
we now proceed to investigate.

The reader of this pamphlet, we trust, will
immediately discover one short argument subver-
sive of this whimsical speculation. It is founded,
we see, upon the assumption that land is the only
source of wealth; a position which we have found
to be altogether untenable. Both manufactures
and commerce are sources, and important sources
of wealth; therefore the landed proprietors are
not the original owners of the whole, nor of
nearly the whole, annual revenue of the country.
The foundation of Mr. Spence's doctrine being

F 2

thus removed, the superstructure of necessity falls to the ground*.

It may be useful, however, to exhibit a fuller and more accurate view of the fallacy of this doctrine respecting consumption. It proceeds entirely upon a misapprehension; upon the confounding together of two things, which are remarkably different, by failing to distinguish the double meaning of an ambiguous term. The two senses of the word *consumption* are not a little remarkable. We say, that a manufacturer consumes the wine which is laid up in his cellar, when he drinks it; we say too, that he has consumed the cotton, or the wool in his warehouse, when his workmen have wrought it up: he consumes part of his money in paying the wages of his footmen; he consumes another part of it in paying the wages of the workmen in his manufactory. It is very evident, however, that consumption, in the case of the wine and the livery servants, means something very different from what it means in the case of the wool or cotton, and the manufacturing servants. In the first.

---

* Mr. Spence here furnishes us with an unanswerable argument against his doctrine of durable commodities. He insists upon it, as we have already seen, that all commerce is unprofitable, which does not import durable commodities. But commodities the more they are durable, are the more opposed to consumption. In conformity with his doctrine of consumption, he ought to recommend commerce in the most perishable commodities. His doctrine of durable commodities affords an argument against his doctrine of consumption; and his doctrine of consumption affords an argument against his doctrine of durable commodities.

case, it is plain, that consumption means extinction, actual annihilation of property; in the second case, it means more properly renovation, and increase of property. The cotton or wool is consumed only that it may appear in a more valuable form; the wages of the workmen only that they may be repaid, with a profit, in the produce of their labour. In this manner too, a land proprietor may consume a thousand quarters of corn a year, in the maintenance of dogs, of horses for pleasure, and of livery servants; or he may consume the same quantity of corn in the maintenance of agricultural horses, and of agricultural servants. In this instance too, the consumption of the corn, in the first case, is an absolute destruction of it. In the second case, the consumption is a renovation and increase. The agricultural horses and servants will produce double or triple the quantity of corn which they have consumed. The dogs, the horses of pleasure, and the livery servants, produce nothing.

We perceive, therefore, that there are two species of consumption; which are so far from being the same, that the one is more properly the very reverse of the other. The one is an absolute destruction of property, and is consumption properly so called; the other is a consumption for the sake of reproduction, and might perhaps with more propriety be called *employment* than consumption. Thus the land proprietor might with more propriety be said to *employ*, than consume the corn, with which he maintains his agricultural horses and servants; but to *consume* the corn which he expends upon his dogs, livery servants, &c. The manufacturer too, would most properly be said to *employ*, not to *consume*, that part of his capital, with which he pays the wages of his manufacturing servants; but to consume in the strictest sense of the word what he expends upon wine, or in maintaining livery servants. Such being the remarkable difference between the meanings of the word consumption, the man in whose reasonings and doctrines those meanings are confounded, must arrive at woeful conclusions.

It appears from this very explanation of the meanings of the term, that it is of importance to the interests of the country, that as much as possible of its annual produce should be *employed*, but as little as possible of it consumed. The whole annual produce of every country is distributed into two great parts; that which is destined to be employed for the purpose of re-production, and that which is destined to be consumed. That part which is destined to serve for reproduction, naturally appears again next year, with its profit. This reproduction, with the profit, is naturally the whole produce of the country for that year. It is evident, therefore, that the greater the quantity of the produce of the preceding year, which is destined to administer to reproduction in the next, the greater will naturally be the produce of the country for that year. But as the whole annual produce of the country is necessarily distributed into two parts, the greater the quantity which is taken for the one, the smaller is the quantity which is left for the other. We have seen, that the greatness of the produce of the country in any year, is altogether dependent upon the greatness of the quantity of the produce of the former year, which is set apart for the business of reproduction. The annual produce is therefore the greater, the less the portion is which is alloted for consumption. If by consumption therefore Mr. Spence means, what we have termed consumption properly so called, or dead unproductive consumption, and it does appear that this is his meaning, his doctrine is so far from being true, that it is the very reverse of the truth. The interests of the country are the most promoted, not by the greatest, but by the least possible consumption of this description.

Let not Mr. Spence, however, be alarmed. Let him rest in perfect assurance, that the whole annual produce of the country will be always very completely consumed, whether his landholders choose to spend or to accumulate. No portion of it will be left unappropriated to the one species of consumption, or to the other. No man, if he can help it, will let any part of his property lie useless and run to waste. Nothing is more clear, than that the self-interest of men, ever has impelled and ever will impel them, with some very trifling exceptions, to use every particle of property which accrues to them, either to the purpose of immediate gratification, or of future profit. That part, however, which is destined for future profit, is just as completely consumed, as

that which is destined for immediate gratification.
A thousand ploughmen consume fully as much
corn and cloth in the course of a year as a regi-
ment of soldiers. But the difference between the
kinds of consumption is immense. The labour
of the ploughman has, during the year, served to
call into existence a quantity of property, which
not only repays the corn and cloth which he has
consumed, but repays it with a profit. The soldier
on the other hand produces nothing. What he
has consumed is gone, and its place is left ab
solutely vacant. The country is the poorer for
his consumption, to the full amount of what he
has consumed. It is not the poorer, but the
richer for what the ploughman has consumed,
because, during the time he was consuming it, he
has reproduced what does more than replace it.

We may hence perceive how it is, that a
country advances in property, and how it is that
it declines. When the produce of each year is
the same with that of the preceding year, it is
plain that the riches of the country are stationary;
when the produce of each year is greater than
that of the preceding, the wealth of the country
is advancing; and when the produce of each year
is less than that of the preceding, the wealth of
the country is on the decline. What then is the
cause by which the annual produce of a country
is increased? About this there can luckily be no
controversy. The cause by which the annual
produce of a country is increased, is the increase
of that division of the annual produce, which is
destined to administer to reproduction. That we

may have more work, we must employ more workmen, and use more materials. The maintenance of these workmen, and the materials on which they operate, are the new fund which is indispensably requisite to the increase of the annual produce. But the only source whence this provision can be drawn, is the source whence the whole fund destined to administer to reproduction is drawn, the annual produce of the country. Now, we have already clearly seen, that the annual produce of every country is always divided into two parts, that which is destined for mere consumption, and that which is destined for the business of reproduction; and that these two parts always wholly exhaust that produce. In whatever proportion, therefore, the part destined for reproduction is augmented, in the same proportion must the part intended for consumption be diminished, and *vice versa*. When the affairs of a country are stationary, when the produce of this year, for example, is the same with that of the last, that is to say, is equal both to that part which was appropriated to the business' of reproduction, and to that which was appropriated to consumption, the part destined for reproduction must have been so large as to suffice for replacing itself, and for affording an increase equal to that part of the annual produce which was taken for consumption. Again, if the produce for the succeeding year is to be the same with the present, such a part of this year's produce must be devoted to the business of reproduction as will suffice to replace itself, and to afford a surplus equal to that part which is reserved for immediate consumption. While this proportion is maintained, the situation of the country is stationary. When, however, it fortunately happens, that a smaller proportion than this of the annual produce is withdrawn for consumption, and a greater proportion than this is left for reproduction, the prosperity of the country advances. The produce of each year is greater than that of the preceding. On the other hand, whenever in the stationary situation of a country, a greater than the usual proportion of the annual produce is withdrawn from the business of reproduction, and devoted to consumption, the produce of the succeeding year becomes necessarily diminished, and as long as this consumption continues, the affairs of the country are retrograde. It is evident, that the arrangement of society, which has a tendency to draw the greatest proportion of the annual produce to consumption, is that in which there is the greatest inequality of fortunes, in which there is the greatest number of persons, who have no occasion to devote themselves to any useful pursuit. But it is the maintenance of great fleets and armies, which is always the most formidable weight in the scale of consumption, and which has the most fatal tendency to turn the balance against reproduction and prosperity. It is by the lamentable continuance of wars, almost always nourished by puerile prejudices and blind passions, that the affairs of prosperous nations are first brought to the stationary condition, and from this plunged into the retrograde,

l

Mr. Spence offers one curious observation. After the statement which we have already quoted, of the miseries which he supposes would flow from a disposition in the landholders not to spend, he anticipates an objection *. Let it not be urged, says he, that what they might save would not be hoarded, (for misers now-a-days are wiser than to keep their money in strong boxes at home) but would be lent on interest; it would still be employed in circulation, and would still give employment to manufacturers. This objection he encounters with the following answer: ' It should ' be considered, that money borrowed on interest ' is destined not for expenditure, but to be em-' ployed as capital; that the very circumstance of ' lessening expenditure decreases the means of ' the profitable employment of capital, and con-' sequently that the employment of the sum al-' luded to as capital, would in no degree diminish ' the hardships of those, who had been deprived ' of the revenue derived from its expenditure.' Wonderful, as after what we have been considering, it may appear, it is yet certain, that Mr. Spence here objects to the augmentation of the portion of the annual produce, which is destined for reproduction. The savings of the landholders, says he, would be employed as capital. But why should they not be employed as capital ? Because, says Mr. Spence, expenditure would be lessened. Well may we here congratulate our author on the clearness and comprehensiveness of his

* See Mr. S's pamphlet, p. 56.

views. What then? The corn which we supposed the landowner to consume upon his agricultural servants and horses, would not be as
completely expended as that which we supposed
him to consume upon his livery servants, his
stud, and his dog kennel? The ploughmen of
the country do not expend as well as the
soldiers? There is here a want of discernment,
which in a man, who stands up as an emphatical
teacher in political economy, does hardly deserve
quarter*. Of the two parts of the annual produce, that which is destined for reproduction and
that which is destined for consumption, the one
is as completely expended as the other, and that
part which is destined for reproduction, is that
which is probably all expended in the shortest
time. For the man who intends to make a profit is

* Here too, Mr. Spence follows a remarkable part of the
system of the original *Economistes*. ' La consommation est la
' mesure de la reproduction.—Plus il se consomme, plus il se
' produit,' said Mercier de la Rivière, Ordre Essentiel des So-
ciétés Polit. Tom. ii. p. 138. At the time when this system.
was first invented, when men had just begun to analyse the
operations of society, such a mistake deserved, perhaps, in-
dulgence. But after the real causes of wealth have been so
clearly evolved by Dr. Smith, after the mysterious process of
production has been so exactly resolved into its first elements,
it shows either a very slight acquaintance with his work, or a
woeful inability to trace the consequences of the truths demonstrated in it, if a man can now adopt the doctrine of the
Economistes respecting consumption.—A late French writer,
M. Say, Economie Polit. Liv. v. ch. 3, tells a pleasant anec-
dote of a practical pupil of this doctrine. " J'ai connu," says
he, " un jeune homme qui fesait voler par la fenêtre les flacons
de cristal a mesure qu'il les vidoit; *il faut*, disait-il, *encourager*
les manufactures."

in haste to obtain it. But a considerable time
may elapse before a man consume the whole of
what he lays up for mere gratification. He may
have in his cellar a stock of wine to serve him for
several years, but the flax or the wool in his warehouse will probably be all worked up in the course
of one year.

To render the futility of Mr. Spence's objection still more clear, we may shew him by an
analysis of a particular case in what manner the
savings of his landholders would contribute not to
the worst but to the best effects in civil society.
As this error respecting the importance of dead
consumption is common both to the mercantile
system and to that of the *Economistes,* and very
generally diffused among the ordinary part of
mankind, it is of no little importance, even at
the risk of being thought tedious, to endeavour
to set it in the strongest light I am able. Let
us suppose that one of Mr. Spence's landholders
with a revenue of £10,000, the whole of which
he has been accustomed to spend in the main-
tainance of a brilliant and luxurious establishment, becomes resolved all at once to cut short
his expenditure one half. He has thus the very
first year £5,000 to dispose of. Even Mr.
Spence allows that he will lend not hoard it.
Let us suppose that he lends it to the linen manufacturer in his neighbourhood. To what use in his
hands is it immediately applied? to the augmentation unquestionably of his business. He goes
directly and buys an additional quantity of flax
from the farmer, he sets to work an additional

number of flax-dressers and spinners, he employs the carpenters, blacksmiths, and other necessary artisans in erecting for him an additional number of looms, and he hires an additional number of weavers. In this manner the £10,000 of the landholder is as completely consumed as ever it was. But £5,000 of it is consumed in a very different manner. It is consumed, 1st upon a very different set of people, and 2d to a very different end. 1. It is consumed upon the growers, the dressers, the spinners, and weavers of flax, with the carpenters, blacksmiths, and other artisans whose labours are subservient to that manufacture, instead of being expended, as formerly, upon lacqueys and cooks, and the other artificers of luxury. 2. It is expended for the sake of reproduction. By means of its expenditure a property of an equal and more than equal amount is now called into existence; by its former expenditure nothing was called into existence. The produce of the country for this year therefore is greater than it would otherwise have been by the amount of £5,000, with its natural profits. If we suppose these profits to be only ten per cent. which is surely reasonable, the produce of the country is thus £5,500 the greater, on account of the very first year's saving of the landholder.*

---

* Mr. Spence says in a note (p. 24 of his pamphlet, 3d edition) 'There is a singular vagueness and confusion in the ' whole of Dr. Smith's reasoning, relative to the different ef- ' fects of prodigality and parsimony upon national wealth. ' His arguments seem to be intended to maintain, that fresh

Another strange perversity of Mr. Spence's doctrine here presents itself. It is directly opposed to the very end which it purposes to promote, consumption. By renouncing Mr. Spence's plan in the instance we have adduced, the country would have more to expend to the amount of £5,500 in the very first year of the new operation of the £5,000; because it would have more produce to the amount of £5,500. Mr. Spence will not surely say that a nation can consume more than it produces; and it is very odd that he and the other pupils of the same doctrine do not reflect that consumption is posterior to production, as it is impossible to consume what is not produced. Consumption in the necessary order of things is the effect of production, not production the effect of consumption. But as every country will infallibly consume to the full amount of its production, whatever is applied to augment the annual produce of the country by consequence augments its annual consumption. The greater therefore the departure from Mr. Spence's rules, the more rapid in every country the increase of consumption will be.*

'capital may be profitably employed, in manufacturing goods 'which nobody will buy; for, certainly no purchasers would 'be found for the goods brought into existence by the employ-'ment of new capital, if all the members of the society were 'to convert the greater part of their revenue into capital.'— This is pretty much as if a follower of the Ptolemaic astronomy should accuse the reasonings of Sir Isaac Newton of vagueness and confusion, because they do not tally with the doctrines of the cycles and epicycles.

* My reader may convince himself by personal inspection

There is another idea the explication of which I could have willingly avoided, because it is more abstruse than may appear adapted to the greater part of the readers of a pamphlet, and after all the pains I can take to render it plain in the narrow space to which I am confined, considerable obscurity may still appear to rest upon it. This explication however is nŏt only necessary because it serves to clear away a remaining objection of the Economistes, but because it exposes the fallacy of certain notions even in this country, which threaten to have very extensive practical consequences. The Economistes and their disciples express great apprehensions lest capital should increase too fast, lest the production of commodities should be too rapid. There is only, say they, a market for a given quantity of commodities, and if you increase the supply beyond that quantity you will be unable to dispose of the surplus.

that the following passage is actually to be found in Mr. Spence's pamphlet, (p. 55) ' Sir Richard Arkwright, by ' his invention and employment of improved machinery, ' in the spinning of cotton, annually gained great riches. ' But would he ever have been wealthy, if he had every year ' spent in tea, wine, sugar, &c. destined for his immediate ' consumption, a sum equal to, or greater than, the whole of ' his gain? Surely not. The dullest intellect must see, that ' he never could have acquired wealth, by this constant ex- ' penditure of his gains, in articles to be consumed by him- ' self, which, when consumed, left no relic behind them; ' however great might have been his gains, and however long ' he might have acted on this system. If, then, a private ' manufacturer cannot acquire wealth in this way, neither can ' a manufacturing nation. The cases are precisely parallel.'

No proposition however in political œconomy seems to be more certain than this which I am going to announce, how paradoxical soever it may at first sight appear; and if it be true, none undoubtedly can be deemed of more importance. The production of commodities creates, and is the one and universal cause which creates a market for the commodities produced. Let us but consider what is meant by a market. Is any thing else understood by it than that something is ready to be exchanged for the commodity which we would dispose of? When goods are carried to market what is wanted is somebody to buy. But to buy, one must have wherewithal to pay. It is obviously therefore the collective means of payment which exist in the whole nation that constitute the entire market of the nation. But wherein consist the collective means of payment of the whole nation? Do they not consist in its annual produce, in the annual revenue of the general mass of its inhabitants? But if a nation's power of purchasing is exactly measured by its annual produce, as it undoubtedly is; the more you increase the annual produce, the more by that very act you extend the national market, the power of purchasing and the actual purchases of the nation. Whatever be the additional quantity of goods therefore which is at any time created in any country, an additional power of purchasing, exactly equivalent, is at the same instant created; so that a nation can never be naturally overstocked either with capital or with commodities; as the very operation of capital

G

makes a vent for its produce. Thus to recur to
the example which we have already analyzed;
fresh goods to the amount of £5,500 were prepared for the market in consequence of the application of the £5000 saved by the landholder.
But what then? have we not seen that the annual
produce of the country was increased; that is, the
market of the country widened, to the extent of
£5,500, by the very same operations? Mr.
Spence in one place advises his reader to consider
the circumstances of a country in which all exchange should be in the way of barter, as the
idea of money frequently tends to perplex. If he
will follow his own advice on this occasion, he
will easily perceive how necessarily production
creates a market for produce. When money is
laid out of the question, is it not in reality the
different commodities of the country, that is to
say, the different articles of the annual produce,
which are annually exchanged against one another? Whether these commodities are in great
quantities or in small, that is to say, whether the
country is rich or poor, will not one half of them
always balance the other? and is it not the barter of
one half of them with the other which actually
constitutes the annual purchases and sales of the
country? Is it not the one half of the goods
of a country which universally forms the market for the other half, and vice versa? And
is this a market that can ever be overstocked?
Or can it produce the least disorder in this market whether the goods are in great or in small
quantity? All that here can ever be requisite is
that the goods should be adapted to one another;

that is to say, that every man who has goods to dispose of should always find all those different sorts of goods with which he wishes to supply himself in return. What is the difference when the goods are in great quantity and when they are in small? Only this, that in the one case the people are liberally supplied with goods, in the other that they are scantily; in the one case that the country is rich, in the other that it is poor: but in the one case, as well as in the other, the whole of the goods will be exchanged, the one half against the other; and the market will always be equal to the supply. Thus it appears that the demand of a nation is always equal to the produce of a nation. This indeed must be so; for what is the demand of a nation? The demand of a nation is exactly its power of purchasing. But what is its power of purchasing? The extent undoubtedly of its annual produce. The extent of its demand therefore and the extent of its supply are always exactly commensurate. Every particle of the annual produce of a country falls as revenue to somebody. But every individual in the nation uniformly makes purchases, or does what is equivalent to making purchases, with every farthing's worth which accrues to him. All that part which is destined for mere consumption is evidently employed in purchases. That too which is employed as capital is not less so. It is either paid as wages to labourers, who immediately buy with it food and other necessaries, or it is employed in the purchase of raw materials. The whole annual produce of the country, therefore,

is employed in making purchases. But as it is
the whole annual produce too which is offered to
sale, it is visible that the one part of it is employed in purchasing the other; that how great
soever that annual produce may be it always
creates a market to itself; and that how
great soever that portion of the annual produce
which is destined to administer to reproduction, that is, how great soever the portion employed as capital, its effects always are to render
the country richer, and its inhabitants more opulent, but never to confuse or to overload the
national market. I own that nothing appears
to me more completely demonstrative than this
reasoning.*

It may be necessary, however, to remark, that a nation may easily have more than enough of any one
commodity, though she can never have more than
enough of commodities in general. The quantity of any one commodity may easily be carried

* The attentive reader will perceive that no deduction
is made in the preceding argument for that part of the annual produce which is consumed immediately by the producer. The motive for this was a desire not to perplex
the argument by qualifying clauses. To notice this particular, at the same time, was entirely unnecessary, since
that part of the annual produce which may be consumed
by the producer, as it increases not the demand in the
national market, so neither does it increase the stock or
supply in that market, because it is not carried to market
at all. It is also to be considered that in every country
where labour is well divided, and skilfully applied, the
proportion of the produce which the producers immediately
consume is always very small.

beyond its due proportion; but by that very circumstance is implied that some other commodity is not provided in sufficient proportion. What indeed is meant by a commodity's exceeding the market? Is it not that there is a portion of it for which there is nothing that can be had in exchange. But of those other things then the proportion is too small. A part of the means of production which had been applied to the preparation of this superabundant commodity, should have been applied to the preparation of those other commodities till the balance between them had been established. Whenever this balance is properly preserved, there can be no superfluity of commodities, none for which a market will not be ready*. This balance too the natural order of things has so powerful a tendency to produce, that it will always be very exactly preserved where the injudicious tampering of government does not prevent, or those disorders in the intercourse of the world, produced by the wars into which the inoffending part of mankind are plunged, by the folly much more frequently than by the wisdom of their rulers.

This important, and as it appears demonstrative doctrine, affords a view of commerce which

---

* What then are we to think of such speculators as Lord Henry Petty, who told the House of Commons in one of the debates on the appropriation of part of the sinking fund in his new finance plan, that it was necessary to prevent the national debt from being paid too fast, lest the country should become overstocked with capital? There was not an individual in the House who contradicted him.

ought to be very consolatory to Mr. Spence. It shews that a nation always has within itself a market equal to all the commodities of which it can possibly have to dispose; that its power of purchasing is always equivalent to its power of producing, or at least to its actual produce; and that as it never can be greater, so it never can be less. Foreign commerce, therefore, is in all cases a matter of expediency rather than of necessity. The intention of it is not to furnish a vent for the produce of the industry of the country, because that industry always furnishes a vent for itself. The intention of it is to exchange a part of our own commodities for a part of the commodities which we prefer to our own of some other nation; to exchange a set of commodities which it peculiarly suits our country to produce for a set of commodities which it peculiarly suits that other country to produce. Its use and advantage is to promote a better distribution, division and application of the labour of the country than would otherwise take place, and by consequence to render it more productive. It affords us a better, a more convenient and more opulent supply of commodities than could have been obtained by the application of our labour within ourselves, exactly in the same manner as by the free interchange of commodities from province to province within the same country, its labour is better divided and rendered more productive.

It thus appears of what extraordinary importance to every community is the augmentation of capital; that is to say, the augmentation of that part of the annual produce which is consumed in the way of reproduction. If we but recall the thought of that important doctrine first illustrated by Smith, that a progression is necessary in national affairs to render the circumstances of the great body of the people in any degree comfortable, our humanity, as well as our patriotism, will become deeply interested in the doctrine of parsimony. Dr. Smith shews that even when a country is stationary, the subsistence of the labouring classes is reduced to the lowest rate which is consistent with common humanity; that is to say, it is barely sufficient to enable them to maintain their present numbers, but not sufficient to enable them in the least degree to augment them. But if we recollect how much greater than this are the powers of multiplication in the species, how natural it is for the average of families to be more numerous than merely to replace the father and the mother; we shall see with feelings of commiseration how wretched must be the circumstances of those families that are more numerous, and of how many human creatures brought into existence, it must be the miserable fate to perish through want of subsistence. But if such is the dismal situation of the great body of the people, when the national affairs are but stationary, how much more shocking to our feelings are their circumstances, when the situation of the country is retrograde! In this situation the labourer is unable to earn even at a rate which is sufficient to maintain the numbers of the labouring class. Calamity now comes down with a heavier hand. That class must even be thinned by the dreadful operation of deficient subsistence! On the other hand, when the affairs of the country are progressive, the wages of the labouring class are sufficient not only to maintain their existing numbers, but to augment them. The reward of labour is liberal. The labourer can support a moderate family with ease; and plenty and comfort diffuse themselves throughout the community. Have we not seen that this progressive state of society, that all these happy consequences result from continual additions made to the capital of the country, or to that part of the annual produce which is devoted to reproduction? and have we not seen that the retrograde condition, with all its deplorable consequences, results from making continual additions to that part of the annual produce which is taken for mere consumption? Little obligation then has society to those doctrines by which this consumption is recommended. Obstacles enow exist to the augmentation of capital without the operation of ridiculous speculations. Were the doctrine that it can increase too fast, as great a truth as it is an absurdity, the experience of all the nations on earth proves to us, that of all possible calamities this would be the least to be feared. Slow has been its progress every where; and low the degree of prosperity which has in any place been given to the mass of the people to enjoy.

CHAP. VII.

Of the National Debt.

WERE the exhortations to consumption, of Mr. Spence and others, addressed only to individuals, we might listen to them with a great deal of indifference; as we might trust with abundant confidence that the disposition in mankind to save and to better their condition would easily prevail over any speculative opinion, and be even little affected by its practical influence. When the same advice, however, is offered to government, the case is widely and awfully changed. Here the disposition is not to save but to expend. The tendency in national affairs to improve, by the disposition in individuals to save and to better their condition, here finds its chief counteraction. Here all the most obvious motives, the motives calculated to operate upon the greater part of mankind, urge to expence; and human wisdom has not yet devised adequate checks to confine within the just bounds this universal propensity. Let us consider then what are likely to be the consequences should this strong disposition become impelled, and precipitated by a prevailing sentiment among mankind. One of the most powerful restraints upon the prodigal inclinations of governments, is the condemnation with which expence, at least beyond the received ideas of propriety, is sure to be viewed by the people. But should this restraint be taken off, should the disposition of government to spend become heated by an opinion that it is right to spend, and should this be still farther inflamed by the assurance that it will by the people also be deemed right in their government to expend, no bounds would then be set to the consumption of the annual produce. Such a delusion could not certainly last long: but even its partial operation, and that but for a short time, might be productive of the most baneful consequences. The doctrines of Mr. Spence which we have already considered, naturally lead to this dangerous application; but it is only when he comes to speak of the national debt that his advice is directly addressed to government.*

'For my own part,' says Mr. Spence,† 'I am

* We have already seen, p. 85, an application of the doctrine of the utility of expence, in the plea of Lord Henry Petty for alienating part of the sinking-fund. The sinking fund has been operating for twenty years. It ought in that time to have given a tolerable specimen of its effects. Well, how has it paid the national debt? Why, the national debt is now nearly triple of what was its amount when the sinking fund was instituted. If the rapid payment of the national debt were the greatest of our dangers, we might bless God upon being the securest nation in the universe! We may here see, however, with some alarm, the extent of practice which might rapidly be given to the consuming doctrine. Lord Henry Petty professes to regard the sinking fund as the sheet anchor of the nation. Yet upon the strength of this speculation he could recommend to Parliament to devote part of that sinking fund to immediate consumption!

† Britain Indep. of Commerce, p. 74.

' inclined to believe that the national debt, instead
' of being injurious, has been of the greatest ser-
' vice to our wealth and prosperity. It appears
' that man is in fact much more inclined to save
' than to spend. The land-proprietors accordingly
' have never fully performed their duty ; they have
' never expended the whole of their revenue.
' What the land-proprietors have neglected to do,
' has been accomplished by the national debt. It
' has every now and then converted twenty or
' thirty millions of what was destined for capital
' into consumable revenue, and it has thus given
' a most beneficial stimulus to agriculture.'

The reader does not, I suppose, expect that I
should compliment this doctrine with any very long
discussion. As it is founded upon the very same
mistakes which we have traced in our author's
doctrines respecting the consumption of individuals; it would be necessary for me to tread over
again the very same steps, to the fatigue of my
reader as well as of myself. As the practical
consequences, however, of these mistakes are
deeply dangerous, and as there is reason to think
that they have a more real operation in the administration of British affairs than the mere speculative reader, it is probable, would easily believe ;
it is necessary to consider with a little attention
the principal points of this application of Mr.
Spence's theory.

According to Mr. Spence the national debt has
been advantageous because the government has
thus spent what the land-proprietors would otherwise have saved. When his language is put into

accurate terms it means this; the land-proprietors have every year endeavoured to increase to a certain amount that part of the annual produce which is destined for the business of reproduction, whereby they would have increased the annual produce, and the permanent riches of the country; but government has every year, or at least at every short interval of years, taken the property which the people would thus have employed in augmenting the riches of the country, and has devoted it to mere dead consumption, whence the increase of production has been prevented. It is in this manner, according to Mr. Spence, that the national debt has been advantageous!

Let us hear Mr. Spence's reasonings in defence of this doctrine. ' Capital,' says he,* ' is es-
' sential to a nation, but a nation may have too
' much of it; for what is the use of capital, but
' to prepare articles on which a revenue may be
' spent, and where is the revenue to be spent, to
' be derived from, if it be all converted into capi-
' tal?' It is evident that Mr. Spence here falls into his old mistake, supposing that capital is not spent as well as revenue, that is, the part of the national produce which is appropriated to reproduction, as well as that which is appropriated to consumption.

' When, during a war,' says Mr. Spence†,
' a loan of twenty or thirty millions is made, in
' what is the sum expended? Is it not consumed

* Britain Indep. of Commerce, p. 75.
† Ibid.

' in providing food and clothing for the army and
' navy, &c.' But, had no loan been wanted; and
had the individuals of the army and navy been
cultivators, manufacturers, and contributors, in
all the necessary ways, to national production,
might not the same sums have been employed in
maintaining and clothing them? The difference
would have been highly important. As industrious
individuals, they would have reproduced within
each year a property equivalent to that which
they consumed, together with its natural profits.
As soldiers and sailors, they consumed without
producing any thing; and at the end of each year
a property equal to what they consumed was destroyed, and not the value of a pin created to
replace it.

After hearing what Mr. Spence has to say in
favour of loans, let us hear him on the subject of
the taxes paid for the interest of those loans.
' These taxes,' says he*, ' are perhaps a greater
' cause of prosperity than the original debt was.'
His reason is immediately added; because, says
he†, ' they are, for the most part, constantly de-
' voted to the purchase of consumable commodi-
' ties;' that is to say, they are constantly devoted
to dead consumption. The same fatal mistake
still clings to Mr. Spence. The double meaning
of the word consumption still confounds him.
Were the sums paid in taxes, not sacrificed to
dead consumption, would they not still be em-

* Britain Indep. of Commerce, p. 75.
† Ibid.

ployed in making purchases? would they not be
employed in purchasing the raw materials of manufactures, or in paying the wages of manufacturing and agricultural servants, who with
these wages again would purchase their food and
clothing? Mr Spence applauds the taxes, because
they take so much from that part of the annual
produce of the country, which is destined for
productive consumption, and add it to the part
which is destined for dead consumption. This is
the very cause for which the intelligent contem-
plator deplores them.

' Heavy taxes,' says Mr. Spence*, ' are doubt-
' less oppressive to many of the members of a
' society individually considered, yet where the
' whole, or by far the greater part of the taxes of
' a nation are expended in that nation, taxation
' may be carried to a very great extent, without
' injuring national prosperity.' It is curious to
observe how extremes meet. This is a favourite
doctrine too of the mercantile system, of which
those of the school of Mr. Spence have so great
an abhorrence. The reason of both is the same,
that the taxes are laid out in the purchase of
commodities; and they have not the discernment
to reflect, that the money would have been as
certainly laid out in the purchase of commodities,
had it remained as capital. As capital, however,
it would within the year have replaced itself with
a profit; as taxes it is all consumed, and nothing
is created to replace it. By its consumption as

* Britain Indep. of Commerce, p. 76.

I

taxes the country is rendered poorer, by its consumption as capital, the country would have become richer.

Mr. Spence has next a most excellent idea. The sums paid as taxes, he allows, might have employed productive labourers. ' But,' says he*, ' if we have already productive labourers, suffi-' cient for the supply of all our wants, why in-' crease their number?' This is an argument the most commodious in the world. It is equally accommodated to all times and places. The population of England and Wales was found, in 1801, to be very nearly nine millions and a half. In the time of Edward the Ist, the population of England and Wales was found to be about two millions and a half. Had Mr. Spence lived in the days of Edward the Ist, his argument would have been just as handy as at the present moment. It would apply as logically to the wilds of Tartary, as to England and France. Let us observe another of Mr. Spence's consistencies. He here tells us, we see, that society ought to become stationary. We have already productive labourers enow; why increase their number? Yet Mr. Spence informed us, in a passage which we have already quoted, that on this increase depended the prosperity of every country. ' A nation,' he told us, ' may be ' said to be in prosperity, which is progressively ' advancing in wealth, where the checks to popu-' lation are few, and where employment and sub-

* Britain Indep. of Commerce, p. 76.

' sistence are readily found for all classes of its
' inhabitants.'

This is all which I can perceive, that Mr.
Spence advances in the form of direct argument,
to prove that the national debt, and heavy taxes,
are a public blessing*; and, if the maxim be well
founded, that the proofs of any proposition ought
to be strong, in proportion as the doctrine is
wonderful, great is the danger that Mr. Spence's
speculations will not have a very splendid fortune †

---

* He refers to Lord Lauderdale's ' Inquiry into the nature
' and origin of public wealth.' His lordship's arguments,
however, are merely those of Mr. Spence extended. They
are drawn from the same source, and applied to the same end.
Wherever the above arguments are conclusive against Mr.
Spence, if they are conclusive against him at all, they are
equally so against Lord Lauderdale. It seems therefore unnecessary to extend the pamphlet by any examination of arguments, which are already refuted.

† Among other accusations which Mr. Spence has brought
against Dr. Smith, he wishes to prove, that, though 'he dis-
sents from the doctrine of the Economistes, he yet ' virtually
' admits its truth.' (See p. 41 of Mr. Spence's pamph. 3d edit.)
' He asserts,' says Mr. Spence, ' that all revenue must be de-
' rived from rent of land, profit of stock, or wages of labour.
' But in the course of his investigation, he admits, that no
' taxes are finally paid by the profit of stock; the employer of
' capital always shifting the burden from himself upon the
' consumer. He allows, too, that taxes cannot finally fall
' upon wages, since the wages of the labourer increase in
' proportion, as the price of the articles he consumes is aug-
' mented by taxation. On what, then, can taxes fall, but
' upon the rent of land? If all revenue be necessarily de-
' rived from rent, wages and profit, and the two latter cannot

There is an idea, however, which he has appended to this doctrine, which would furnish occasion to a most important inquiry; were it not of a more extensive nature, than to admit of being brought within the limits of the present Tract. ' In the time of war,' says Mr. Spence *, ' when the most taxes are paid, the bulk of the ' population of this country enjoy greater pros- ' perity than at any other time.' He adds, ' just ' now, for example, nevei were the bulk of ' the people so prosperous.' As he states this merely as an inference from his theory, entirely unsupported by any reference to facts, and as we have seen that his theory is extremely erroneous, we might reject the inference without any farther inquiry. But I am desirous of entering my protest in a manner somewhat more circumstantial against an opinion demonstratively unfounded, cruel to the sufferers, and calculated, as far as its influence extends, to prolong the national ca-

' be affected by taxation, Dr. Smith, on his own premises, ' admits the truth of the doctrine of the Economists.' One can with some difficulty determine what to say of this. It is directly untrue. Dr. Smith is so far from saying, that no taxes fall ultimately either upon the profit of stock or the wages of labour, that he explains particularly in what manner taxes *do* fall upon both. Mr. Spence, however, certainly did not intend this misrepresentation. He tells us, that he borrowed the idea from the Edinburgh Review. It is probable, that he trusted to this authority, without undergoing the drudgery of consulting Dr. Smith; (taking the business of instructing the public very easily!) and the writer in the Review, with the precipitance natural to a reviewer, must have made the assertion at random.

* Britain Indepen. of Commerce, p. 76.

H

lamity of war; an opinion the more likely, if false, to produce disastrous consequences, because it is entertained by many persons in the more affluent circumstances of life, for whom it is too natural to believe, when they themselves are at their ease, that all the world are in a similar situation. It must have been from such a consideration as this of the circumstances of the poor, from an attentive inquiry founded upon his own enjoyments, that Mr. Spence must have learned to assure us, that they are in great prosperity. Surely, Mr. Cobbett will here take up arms against his new confederate. There is no point which Mr. Cobbett has laboured with greater industry, and better effect, for many months, than to prove that the situation of the lower orders has become much more unfavourable since the commencement of Mr. Pitt's career as a minister. I remember some time ago, though the date I cannot assign, he presented to us a calculation to prove how much the price of the quartern loaf had risen upon the wages of the labourer, and how inadequate his weekly wages had now become, to afford even bread, (not to speak of fire, clothing, and lodging, or a day of sickness) even to a moderate family. To afford evidence upon this subject, sufficient to compel the assent of such persons as are resolved to withhold it as long as they possibly can, a very copious induction of well attested facts would be requisite. These on such a question could not be very easily procured; and the inquiry, even if the facts were ascertained, would extend itself beyond

the limits to which we are at present confined.
We can, however, appeal within a narrow compass to a few general facts, which afford a strong
ground for inference to the whole subject. One
of these, of a most extraordinary and important
nature, is the state of the poor's rate. The
medium average of the annual expenditure on
account of the poor, in the years 1783, 1784, and
1785, was £2,004,238. During the period of
peace, which intervened from this date till the
breaking out of the war in 1793, no general
account was taken of the poor's rate; and we
have, therefore, no complete collection of facts,
by which we can ascertain in what degree it increased during that period. If we may form,
however, a conclusion from the general state of
the country, in which wages were continually advancing, while the price of provisions was stationary, or rather on the decline, we seem
warranted to infer, that it did not increase at all,
if it did not rather decline; at any rate that it did
not increase, but in a very small degree. We
have something indeed much more precise than
this, on which to found our conclusions. In the
Returns from the Parishes inserted in the Work
of Sir F. M. Eden, on the Poor, we have statements of the annual expenditure during that
period; and though they are not digested into
tables, or the general results exhibited, a comparison in a few cases will satisfy the inquirer,
that the poor's rate was the same, or very nearly
the same, in 1785 and 1792. The case, how-

ever, widely altered during the progress of the war. The attention of the nation had been gradually more and more attracted to this growing calamity during some years previous to 1803, when an act of the legislature was passed, for taking an account of the nature and amount of the expenditure on the poor. At this time it was found to amount to the enormous sum of £4,267,965, 9s. 2d. In the course of ten years of war, therefore, the poor's rate had more than doubled. In nine years, from 1776 to 1785, it had increased only £473,434; in ten years, from 1793 to 1803, it increased £2,263,727. Does this fact seem to support the strange conclusion of Mr. Spence, that the people of England are most prosperous during war? and above all, that they were never in so prosperous a condition, as they are at this moment? Does Mr. Spence really know, that the number of persons in England, who receive parochial charity, is 1,234,768? The whole population, exclusive of military and convicts, but including the paupers, are 8,872,980. Deduct from this the number of paupers, we have 7,638,212. The paupers, therefore, are to the rest of the population, as one to six nearly. If we suppose, that the higher and middling classes form but one fourth of the population, we shall find that nearly every fifth individual in the labouring classes is a parish pauper. Does this lamentable and extraordinary fact indicate a state of prosperity? If we consider that it is the male part of the population chiefly, that is the earning part and pays the poor's rate, it will appear, that the paupers are equal to nearly one third of the whole male population, including old men, young men, or children. Mr. Spence will here, it is probable, launch out into a declamation on the growing vices of the poor, (this at least is the general resource) and will to these ascribe the extraordinary increase of the poor's rate during the war. But why should the vices of the poor have increased so fast during the war? If this is the effect of war, deeply is its prolongation to be. deplored. I know, however, no *facts* by which it can be made appear, that the poor are more vicious than they were in 1785; and as to complaints, these were as strong fifty years ago, as they are now. If it be said, that the poor's rate itself is a proof of the increase in the vices of the poor; this is merely begging the question. It is first making the vices of the poor account for the poor's rate, and next the poor's rate account for the vices. Besides, how much soever the growing tendency of vice is to be deplored, its progress in a whole people is always much slower than what is here ascribed to it. The comparison too of the wages of the labourer, with the price of provisions, as made by Mr. Cobbett, in the manner stated above, affords direct evidence on this subject, and leads to the same lamentable conclusion. There are, unluckily, but few recent statements publicly attested, to which on this subject a writer can appeal, and I am unwilling to advance any thing merely on my own experience and observation. There are, however, some general facts which afford a fair inference to all other cases. In some papers for example printed in 1807, by order of the society of shipowners in Great Britain, I find it stated, that since the year 1780, the price of provisions has increased £84, 8s. 2d. per cent. That wages, however, have increased only £39, 7s. 1d. per cent. a rate of increase which is not nearly one half of that of provisions. This account too of the low rate of wages is the more to be depended upon, that it was adverse to the conclusion which the ship owners wanted to establish. Now, though the shipping trade has been far from flourishing, there has been no diminution in the employment of shipwrights, because the enormous demand in the king's yards, and in the navy, has much more than compensated for any slackness in the yards of the merchants. We have never heard complaints, that shipwrights were not as well paid as any other artificers of a similar description; that their wages have not risen in a similar, or rather in a superior proportion. We may, therefore, infer, with abundant assurance, that the rate of wages in proportion to that of provisions, has in all cases where some peculiar circumstances have not created an extraordinary competition for hands, suffered a similar depression. From all this we are surely authorised to conclude, that the assertion of Mr. Spence respecting the prosperous condition of the people at large, is rash and unwarranted.

I am unwilling to dwell upon this topic, as I am sensible, that I expose myself to a very formidable argument, which we have acquired, in this country, a wonderful dexterity in wielding against one another, that is, the *argumentum ad invidiam*, (if Mr. Cobbett will for once pardon the use of a learned phrase) the argument, not of refutation, but of odium. The opinion which I have just now ventured to express, and which, if true, it is of so much importance not only to express but to proclaim, there are many gentlemen, who will ingeniously refute not by attacking the argument, but the author; not by showing that the opinion is unfounded, but by asserting, that the author wishes to stir up the poor against the rich. The two antagonists whom I have more particularly challenged in this tract, I must, however, deny the honour of belonging to that illustrious body. If my argument has not convinced them, they may, if they deem it of sufficient importance, endeavour to refute it; but both of them seem to be too much fettered by old fashioned prejudices, to satisfy themselves, that it is the best mode of refuting an argument to calumniate the arguer.

It might be not useless to those who are the most averse to hear of the fact, barely to allow themselves for one moment to suppose it real, and then to ask themselves, whether it ought to be disguised or to be made known; whether the fatal cause is most likely to be removed by concealment or by exposure. That the fact, if real, is a lamentable one, I suppose will not be doubted; first on principles of mere humanity, next on those of patriotism. For what would it indicate? Have we not seen that when a country is prosperous, the labouring classes of the people are by necessary consequence in comfortable circum-stances ? that when the comforts of the labouring classes have decayed, the prosperity of the coun-try is at least at a stand, a point from which de-clension is the consequence, natural and very dif-ficult to be avoided ? Since the subject is then of so much importance, let us hope that all those whom the opinion here stated may offend, will exert themselves to refute it. If they can pro-duce facts, but nearly as strong against it as are stated to prove it, our wishes will forcibly incline us all to range ourselves of their party.

General Reflections.

AFTER this controversy to determine whether any wealth is derived from commerce, the ques-tion respecting its relative importance, as a source of production, is of some moment. If it is not altogether destitute of utility, in what degree ought it to be considered as valuable ? Though Mr. Spence, who condemns it as entirely unpro-ductive, is excluded from this inquiry, it is a sub-ject on which our countrymen have need of much more instruction than it will be possible to give them in a few pages of this pamphlet.

A general idea of the value of commerce, as a source of wealth, may be easily derived from the doctrines which have been laid down in the prece-ding discussion. We have seen that the true con-

ception of a nation's wealth is that of her powers
of annual production. A nation is poor or is rich
according as the quantity of property which she
annually creates, in proportion to the number of
her people, is great or is small. Now commerce
tends to increase this annual produce by occasion-
ing a more productive application and distribution
both of the land and of the labour of the country.
Instead of raising flax, for example, or hemp,
on our land, we raise corn; with that corn we
feed a number of hardware manufacturers, and
with this hardware we buy a greater quantity of
flax than the land which raised our corn, and fa-
bricated our hardware, would have produced.
This is exactly equivalent to an increase in the
powers of our land; it is the same thing as if we
had been enabled to make that portion of land
which could only raise a certain quantity of flax,
raise all that additional quantity which our hardware could purchase. In this instance, the increase in the productive powers of the country by
the mercantile operations we have supposed,
seems to be measured by the gains of the merchant. The gains of the merchant, however,
may be considered in different lights. First he
may be enabled to sell the whole of the imported
flax at as high a rate as that at which the flax
raised at home could afford to be sold. If he can
sell it at this rate, his gains seem to measure the
increase in the annual produce very exactly; they
are the price of the additional quantity of flax
which his hardware has purchased. But, se-
condly, if these gains are very high, competitors

will be attracted, who will endeavour to share in them by reducing the price of what they import. In this case, if the quantity imported remained the same, the gains of the merchants being reduced, the increase of the annual produce would surpass the gains of the merchants. There is, however, a third light in which the subject is to be viewed; this reduction in the price of flax would render it impossible any longer to raise it with a profit on a considerable part of the land which had been formerly devoted to it; only such land as had a peculiar adaptation to the crop could now be cultivated for it; the quantity imported would therefore be increased; but though the profits of the merchants would thus be multiplied, a fresh addition would be made by every increase of the importation to the annual produce of the country, whence it would appear that in this case too the gains of the merchants would fall below the increase afforded to the nation. There is a fourth case, which requires no illustration, in which, by means of monopoly and bounties, the gains of the merchant may be very high, when those of the country are very low, in which the merchant may gain when the country loses. But in all cases in which trade is free, the gain to the country cannot be less than the profit to the merchant; in almost all such cases it must be greater.

From this view of the subject it will be seen that no exact estimate can be made of what any nation gains by commerce. It may, however, be safely concluded that its importance is in general greatly overrated. Every arm could be employed, and every article of the annual produce could be sold, if the country were surrounded by Friar Bacon's wall of brass, a thousand feet high. The labour of the nation would not be so productive; the annual produce would not be so large; the people would not be so cheaply, that is, liberally supplied with commodities; neither individuals, nor the government, could spend so much without turning back the progress of the country. But every labourer would find work, and every shilling of capital would find employment.

When we hear people, therefore, talk, as we do too often hear them, and in places too high, of commerce as the cause of our national grandeur; when we find it appealed to as the measure of our prosperity; and our exports and our imports quoted as undeniable proofs that the country has flourished under the draining of the most expensive war that ever nation waged on the face of the earth, we have reason to smile at the ignorance or the deceitfulness of the speaker. Further, when we find important measures of state embraced upon the allurements of these ideas, when regulations are formed to bend forcibly the national industry to a conformity with them; but above all, when wars are commenced, or peace is repelled, for the loss or gain, or rather much more frequently an absurd apprehension respecting the loss or gain of a branch of commerce, we ought to deplore the fate of the nation, and the unskilfulness of her rulers. We may assert, without an hyperbole, that the fee simple of our whole export commerce is not worth the expence of the last fifteen years war ; that had it all been sacrificed, to the last sixpence, to save us from that expence, we should have been gainers by the bargain.* Had Mr. Spence then directed his efforts to moderate our ideas of the value of commerce, without teaching other doctrines which, first, were false, and next led to practical conclusions of the most dangerous tendency, he might have been of service to his country. It is but too true that the greater number of the persons with whom we converse seem to imagine that commerce creates wealth by a sort of witchcraft, as our financiers would sometimes persuade us

---

* This may be rigidly proved by arithmetical demonstration. Let us take our commerce at its present standard. We export rather more than forty millions a year of British produce and manufactures. Let us suppose that one-fourth of this is gain to the country, which is probably a good deal more than the fact. The annual gain of the nation by this trade is then £10,000,000. Now the most steady and flourishing kinds of business are seldom worth more than ten years purchase. But we shall make a much larger allowance. Land itself is only worth thirty years purchase even at its present elevated price; and commerce is surely worth one-third less than land. Let us suppose then that our commerce is worth 20 years purchase; while our land is worth 30. The whole of our commerce, even at this high estimate, would be worth only £200,000,000. But we have added by the war above £300,000,000 to the national debt. When we consider that the war taxes were taken at £21,000,000 in Lord Henry Petty's budget for one year only, we may be pretty certain we are below the mark, when we say at a venture that £100,000,000 more have been raised for the war by that means. It thus appears that the war with the French revolution has already cost us more than twice the worth of our whole commerce !

that they can maintain fleets and armies by a juggle of figures. The truth is, that nothing creates wealth but the hands of our industrious countrymen, set to work by the means, and regulated by the skill and judgment of others. Commerce is only one of the causes, and one not very high in the scale, by which their industry is rendered more productive.

Mr. Cobbett's antipathy to commerce appears to me to be founded on juster views than the disapprobation of Mr. Spence. Little troubling himself about the subtle question of the origin of wealth, and unacquainted with the plausible and ingenious, but fallacious arguments of the *Economistes*, he yet saw clearly, and felt keenly, the injury which the country sustained from a policy guided by ideas of the boundless value of commerce. It is from topics of this sort that almost all his invectives against commerce are drawn. ‘ Wars’, he cries,* ‘ have been made over and ‘ over again for the sake of commerce ; and when ‘ the rights and honour of the nation are to be ‘ sacrificed by a peace, the regaining or preserv- ‘ ing of commerce is invariably the plea. To ‘ support commerce, the wars in Egypt were un- ‘ dertaken; the wars in India are carried on with- ‘ out ceasing; the war in South-America and in ‘ Africa are now undertaken. Oh! What Eng- ‘ lish blood, and English labour, and English hap- ‘ piness, and English honour, has not this com- ‘ merce cost!’ Thus again, he says,† ‘ The fact

'is, that the means of supporting fleets and ar-
'mies, the means of meeting all the squander-
'ings that we witness, the means of paying the
'dividends at the bank, *come out of the land of
'the country and the labour of its people.* Nothing
'is more convenient for the purpose of a squan-
'dering, jobbing, corrupting, bribing minister,
'than a persuasion amongst the people, that it is
'from *the commerce,* and not from *their labour,*
'that the taxes come ; and it has long been a fa-
'shionable way of thinking, that it is no matter
'how great the expences are, so that the com-
'merce does but keep pace with them in every
'case. Nothing can better suit such a minister
'and his minions, than the propagation of opi-
'nions like these. But, gentlemen, you have
'seen the commerce tripled since the fatal day
'when Pitt became minister ; and have you found
'that *your* taxes *have not been increased?* The
'commerce has been tripled, and so have the
'parish paupers. Away, then, I beseech you
'with this destructive delusion ! See the thing in
'its true light. Look upon *all* the taxes as ari-
'sing out of *the land and the labour,* and distrust
'either the head or the heart of the man who
'would cajole you with a notion of their arising
'from any other source.' Once more, ' If events,'
says he,* ' proceed as, thank God, they are now
'proceeding, this so long deluded people will
'think rightly upon the subject of commerce,
'and when they do, away go, in a very short

* Cobbett's Political Register, p. 824.

' space of time, all the locusts that now eat up
' our substance; that now degrade the country;
' that now barter its happiness and its honour for
' their own villainous advantage. England has
' long groaned under a *commercial system*, which
' is the most oppressive of all possible systems;
' and it is, too, a quiet, silent, smothering op-
' pression, that it produces, which is more hateful
' than all others.'

But Mr. Cobbett should consider that commerce is entirely innocent of that political misconduct which excites his complaint and indignation. If an ignorant minister is deceived into absurd measures by overrating the value of commerce, or a deceitful minister screens his administration by disseminating exaggerated ideas of
its value, the fault is with such ministers. How
is commerce to blame? The argument which Mr.
Cobbett uses against commerce is exactly the
same with that which is used by infidels against
religion. Because courts and ministers have so
often founded on religious pretexts measures the
most pernicious to human kind, they conclude
that religion ought to be abolished. Their complaints run entirely in Mr. Cobbett's strain.
What wars, say they, and bloodshed has it occasioned? What chains has it forged for mankind?
True, we answer. The mischief which has been
wrought, in the name of religion, has been infinite and detestable. The effects of religion,
meanwhile, like the efforts of commerce, are all
beneficent. But were both religion and commerce extinguished, can Mr. Cobbett, or the in-

fidels, imagine that ignorant ministers would not still mistake their duty, and mercenary ministers not find pretexts to delude the people ? Let us only consult the most vulgar experience. France has no commerce, nor Austria, the boasted value of which can impose upon the public. But are Austria and France governed with any more attention to the happiness of the people than England ? and are ministers there without their pretexts to persuade the people that they are well governed, as well as the ministers of England ? Have not the rulers of France, the glory of the nation and its renown in arms, of which they make abundant use? This too used to be the boast of Austria. At present it is laid aside for a space. But the preservation of the independence of their country, the dignity of its royal family, and of its nobles, is still in Austria a source of triumph and a claim of merit. The fact is, that nothing is a security against deception, but the knowledge of the people, by which it is detected. As long as a people are ignorant enough to be easily deceived, it is not in the nature of human affairs that deception should not take place ; it would be absurd to expect it. Let Mr. Cobbett rest assured that wherever a nation has been so far deficient in knowledge as to be deluded into the approbation of impolitic measures by boasts respecting commerce, it would have been no difficult matter to have found the means of deceiving it, had commerce not existed. I am far therefore from concluding with Mr. Cobbett that, were commerce gone, we should be delivered from ' all the

' locusts that now eat up our substance.' Could the loss of commerce so enlighten us that we should be proof against delusion? Or are the means of deception so few that they are all summed up in commerce?

Mr. Cobbett appears to imagine that commerce has corrupted our government. It has subjected us, he says, to oppression. But as he does not explain how, it is not easy to reply to this objection. As Mr. Cobbett is far from supposing, that the popular part of our government has lately increased in power, commerce must have disordered the constitution, by increasing the power, either of the kingly or of the aristocratical part. This is directly contrary to the opinion of Mr. Spence, who explains at considerable length* the tendency of commerce to break the force of regal and aristocratical servitude. The regal and aristocratical power in this country has increased by the amazing increase of the share of the annual produce which is placed at the disposal of the executive government, and which is chiefly distributed among the great men. But it is the parliament by which this amazing increase has been voted. Now commercial men, though their number in parliament is considerable, form but a small proportion to the whole; neither have we ever heard that they were more forward in voting the taxes than the landlords and gentlemen. The fact is, that though rich merchants and manufacturers are by far too apt to ape their betters

* See Brit. Indep. Com. p. 20 to 26.

in a foolish predilection for arbitrary principles of government in regard to the great body of the people, yet their situation does lead them to an intercourse with the lower orders upon rather more liberal terms than the situation of the mere land proprietor. The persons employed by the merchant and the manufacturer are in general very independent of their employers, and if they meet with ill usage, will immediately change their masters. Those on the other hand, who are under the land proprietor, are in general far more dependent upon him; and his situation in this manner generally creates in him a much more arbitrary temper and conduct. He is therefore almost always disposed to coercive and arbitrary measures of government; and were his prejudices to influence the tone of administration, absolute power would seldom fail to be the final result. Even some of the prejudices connected with commerce have been extremely favourable to liberty in this country. The supposition that the country depended in a great degree upon commerce, and the vast instrumentality of the lower orders in this department, have contributed greatly to the consideration of their interests in our course of legislation. Had the body of our population consisted entirely of the tenants and peasants of the landholders, and our legislature consisted of none but the latter, the more completely subservient the tenants and peasants could have been rendered to their masters, the more happy a situation of things it would have appeared. Mr. Cobbett's opinion is contradicted by the whole of our experience. All over

Europe where the population has chiefly consisted of landholders and peasants, arbitrary power and poverty have invariably reigned. In Great Britain, where commerce has been established, much more freedom and opulence have been enjoyed.

Were our attention much more concentrated upon domestic industry, and a far less proportion devoted to foreign trade, Mr. Cobbett thinks the national interests would be promoted. There is reason, to some extent, for his opinion. Agricultural industry is not at the same height in England as commercial and manufacturing industry. But what is the reason of this? It is chiefly owing to the distribution of our landed property. The greater part of it is possessed in portions too large. A man of ample capital will never lay it out in cultivating another man's estate; because this employment is less independent; because it is a station of inferiority. He therefore, in preference devotes his fortune to trade. The cultivation of the ground is discouraged too, by the imposts of tithes, and of poor rates; which are taxes upon improvement. By these, and various other causes, capital is drawn from agriculture. But is this the fault of commerce? It only takes what impolitic and unnatural laws will not permit the other to employ.

Commerce, then, we may infer from all that has been said, is a very good thing when it comes spontaneously, but a thing which may very easily be bought too dear. The two main springs of national wealth and prosperity, are the cultivation of the land, and manufactures for home em-

ployment and consumption. Foreign commerce
is a mere auxiliary to these two; and its sole utility consists in enabling the nation to obtain its
supply to certain demands, at a less expence of
land and labour than it could have supplied them
at home. It may be clearly seen too, that it depends upon the circumstances of other nations, in
what degree foreign commerce may be advantageous. When the nations which surround England, for example, are so situated that certain articles which England affords bear in them a very
high price, while many other articles in them
which England wants bear a very low price, it
suits England to manufacture a great deal for
foreign markets, because, with a small quantity of
what she produces, she can supply herself with a
great quantity of what they produce. But should
those articles in the surrounding countries gradually become dearer, while the articles from
England become cheaper, it would then become
less and less the interest of England to manufacture for these countries; and if the articles which
she wants should rise in them to the price at
which she could provide them from her own land
and labour, it would then become her interest to
provide them at home, and manufacture for these
countries no longer. The fluctuations then of
foreign commerce, afford a very fallacious indi-
cation of national prosperity. The national prosperity may in some cases even be consulted by
abstaining from it.

After forming these conclusions respecting the
sources of production, one great branch of the

subject of which we have treated in this pamphlet, some remaining reflections yet force themselves upon us respecting its other great branch, consumption ; concerning which the misapprehensions of our countrymen are not less numerous, and are still more nearly allied to practice.

Notwithstanding the avidity for immediate gratification, with which the greater part of mankind appear to be inspired, the disposition to accumulate seems, from experience, to be a still more powerful propensity ; and wherever men are secure in the enjoyment of their property, a great part of them always exert themselves to make what they get exceed what they spend. By means of this powerful principle it is natural for every nation, which has scope for its industry, to make continual advancement, to see the produce of every succeeding year surpass that of the year that went before it. One arrangement of society may be more favourable to this advancement than another. In one country the natural subdivision of property may be more counteracted than in another. But no arrangement of society, consistent with any tolerable degree of freedom and security, seems capable of preventing this wonderful agent from adding something every year to the fund of production, from continually increasing the annual produce. As it is this gradual produce on which the happiness of the great body of the people depends, we may reflect with satisfaction and wonder on the strength of the principle on which it is secured ; on the provision which is laid in the original laws of human nature for the well-being of the species!

But when we contemplate this beneficent arrangement, and afterwards turn our eyes to the actual state of things among mankind, it is impossible not to be struck with grief and amazement. From the operation of so powerful and steady a principle we should every where have expected opulence and prosperity; we actually behold, almost every where, poverty and wretchedness! Where are we to find the solution of this strange contradiction in human affairs? By whom is that property devoured which mankind, in their individual capacity, have so strong an inclination to increase?

The general expensiveness of government, of which complaints are so common, and so well founded, will not account for the fact. All governments constantly spend as much as ever the people will let them. An expensive government is a curse. Every farthing which is spent upon it, beyond the expence necessary for maintaining law and order, is so much dead loss to the nation, contributes so far to keep down the annual produce, and to diminish the happiness of the people. But where a nation is considerable, and its industry improved and productive, the mere expence of government, however prodigal, cannot bear a great proportion to the whole of the annual produce; and the general savings of all the individuals in the nation can hardly fail to surpass the expences of the court. A country therefore can hardly fail to improve, notwithstanding the ordinary expence even of a wasteful government; it will only improve more slowly than it would have done had the government been more economical. The people may be still prosperous and happy, though they might have been a little more prosperous and happy, had the expence of the government been less.

To what baneful quarter, then, are we to look for the cause of the stagnation and misery which appear so general in human affairs ? War ! is the answer. There is no other cause. This is the pestilential wind which blasts the prosperity of, nations. This is the devouring fiend which eats up the precious treasure of national economy, the foundation of national improvement, and of national happiness. Though the consumption even of a wasteful government cannot keep pace with the accumulation of individuals, the consumption of war can easily outstrip it. The savings of individuals, and more than the savings of individuals, are swallowed up by it. Not only is the progression of the country stopped, and all the miseries of the stationary condition are experienced, but inroads are almost always made upon that part of the annual produce which had been previously devoted to reproduction. The condition of the country therefore goes backwards; and in general it is only after the country is so exhausted that the expence of the war can hardly by any means be found, that it is ever put an end to. When the blessing of peace is restored, the country slowly recovers itself. But hardly has it gained its former prosperity when it is generally re-struck by the calamity of war, and compelled to measure back its steps. In this alternation between misery and the mere beginnings of prosperity, are nations for the most part, condemned to remain; the energies of human nature are exerted to no purpose; its beneficent laws are counteracted; and the happiness of society, which seems to be secured by such powerful provisions, like the water of Tantalus, is only allowed to approach the lip, that it may be immediately dashed away from it. The celebrated Vauban, the unrivalled engineer of Louis the 14th, whose profession made him locally acquainted with every part of his country, and who spoke the language of an honest observation, untainted by the prejudices of his education, or the course of his life, observed, ' Si la France est si misérable, ce n'est ni à l'in- ' temperie de l'air, ni à la faute des peuples, ni à ' la stérilité des terres, qu'il faut l'attribuer ; puis- ' que l'air y est excellent, les habitans laborieux, ' adroits, pleins d'industrie et très nombreux ; ' *mais aux guerres qui l'ont agitée depuis long-* ' *tems et au defaut d'économie que nous n'enten-* ' *dons pas assez.*'*

In every country, therefore, where industry is free, and where men are secure in the enjoyment of what they acquire, the greatest improvement which the government can possibly receive is a steady and enlightened aversion to war. While such a nation remains at peace, the faults of the

* Vauban Dixme Royale.

government can hardly ever be so great, that the merits of the nation will not more than compensate them, and that society from its own beneficent tendency will not improve. Nothing however can compensate the destruction of war. The creative efforts of individuals can never equal its gigantic consumption, and the seeds of prosperity are eaten up.

Clear and striking as these truths appear, we may surely indulge the belief that it is not impossible to impress them pretty deeply both upon governments and people ; for in the history of wars we seldom find that the people have been less infatuated, or less to blame than their rulers. If we analyse too the causes of all the wars which are on record, we shall find reason to conclude, that it is by no means so difficult a thing to avoid wars as it is generally supposed. In by far the greater number of cases, both parties have been to blame, and a little more wisdom on either side might have averted the calamity.

From these general considerations respecting war, our thoughts are forcibly attracted to a particular case, deeply affecting the interests of us all, the war in which we are at present engaged. The question which the foregoing reflections most particularly suggest is, " Whether we cannot now get out of it ?" But were this question determined in the affirmative, a very difficult task would still remain, to persuade the people of this country that they might rely upon the demonstration. A portion of them, by no means inconsiderable either for numbers or influence, seem bent to believe, and government appears well disposed to encourage the belief, that we cannot bring it to a period. It is important however to ask these persons, whether they can point out a time when there is any probability that we can put an end to it more advantageously? If they shew us any certain object of great importance which by continuing the war for one year longer we may be sure of obtaining, we might listen to them, and weighing carefully the object to be obtained with one year's expence of the war, determine whether it is worth that expence. With great assurance, however, might we determine that if the object were not one of the very greatest importance, as well as its attainment very certain, the question about continuing the war did not deserve a moment's consideration. But if no desirable object whatever can be pointed out for which we are called upon to fight; if we are called upon to fight not for one year or two years, but for any number of years, to obtain an indescribable something; if there is no probability that any number of years fighting, that can be named, can place us in a situation to obtain one object more than we can obtain at this moment; of what sort is the advice that would urge us to continue the war? When men engage in any scheme, they in general desire to know that the chance of gain is greater than the chance of loss; all serious undertakings which are not of this description every prudent man avoids; even the rashest men will not embark in a project in which they cannot persuade themselves that

5

the chance of gain is at least equal to the chance of loss. A project in which the loss is certain, but in which an adequate gain is so far from certain, that there is no gain whatever of which even a hope can be formed, is not a choice for persons in the exercise of reason.

We confidently assume that the advocates of war can point out no time at which there is the smallest probability we can terminate the war with more advantage than we can at the present. Britain and France seem now to be come to that position in which neither can any longer do much harm to the other. France can do nothing to affect our maritime superiority, and we can do nothing to affect her superiority on land. The two countries may persist in wasting each other, and perpetuating the misery of their respective populations; they may render each other posi-tively weaker as well as more wretched, but neither will have gained any relative advantage, because the causes of decline in both will operate equally. Can we land an army in Europe that shall beat in the forces of France, and reduce her bounda-ries to that circumference which suits our ideas of propriety? Is it recommended to us to continue warring with France till the moment we can atchieve this glorious enterprise? Is this what the advocates for war mean when they tell us we must fight till we can obtain a secure and honourable peace? It is of infinite consequence they should define to us their ideas. While men confine themselves to vague and general phrases, their meaning can never be known to others, and is seldom known to themselves. A secure and honourable peace may signify any thing. I can conceive a situation of circumstances in which it would be held to mean nothing less than the expulsion of Bonaparte from France, and the restoration of the Bourbons; I can conceive another situation of circumstances in which it would be made to signify the surrender of our fleet and the resignation of Ireland.

If the advocates for war would condescend to define, I believe they would not say that we ought to fight till we can send an army to the continent capable of vanquishing France; they would certainly on the other hand allow that the nature of our country, and the amount of its population, render the hope of such an event altogether ridiculous. If this prospect then is relinquished, to what object next shall we direct our expectations ? Shall we wait till a general combination of princes on the continent, with an overwhelming force, has reduced the power of Bonaparte to a size which will let our fears go to rest ? Long and obstinately have we adhered to this expectation. The course of events has at last, however, produced a state of things in which the most pertinacious must surrender this strong hold. It is impossible that experience can afford a demonstration more complete than it has afforded against any hope which can be raised upon a combination of princes against France. Four times within the last twenty years have formidable combinations of this kind been formed. Four times has France completely subdued them. At each time has she extended her influence over an additional portion of Europe. Nearly the whole of it is at last submitted to her imperial dictates. When the power of Europe was entire, and that of France was in its infancy, could France easily subvert the greatest confederacies? When the power of Europe is entirely broken, and that of France has grown to a gigantic size, are we to expect that she will suffer by them?

If we cannot entertain the hope of being able to terminate the war with more advantage, either from the ability of Britain to subdue Bonaparte, or that of a confederacy of European princes; to what other event are we to look? The death of Bonaparte? This will no doubt happen sooner or later. It may not, however, happen for thirty years to come. Bonaparte is yet but a young man. He enjoys good health. He is extremely temperate, and takes a great deal of exercise. His mind has been subject to much agitation, but a period of calm may now be expected. Besides, it is not always found that agitation of mind has a tendency to shorten life. Aurengzebe, the celebrated emperor of Indostan, who had to wade, by usurpation, through the blood of his family, to the throne, who was a man of a weak constitution, and who continued engaged in an almost perpetual scene of war and disquietude, lived, in a climate not favourable to longevity, till beyond the age of eighty. Were we however assured that the life of Bonaparte would not be long, what assurance can we possibly have that the change would be in our favour? Let this point be thoroughly ascertained. The present is a case too serious to satisfy ourselves with childish suppositions. We ought to have proof, undeniable proof, that the change would be advantageous, highly advantageous; and also that it is near, before on such a plea, we consent to the lamentable consumption of a protracted war. On this subject again what is the lesson that experience, the true and faithful counsellor of nations, teaches? That the change would not be for our advantage. The government of France has undergone three or four changes since in 1793 we began to contend with it. Whatever was its existing state, we always hoped that the next change would bring some wonderful alteration in our favour. Change, however, succeeded change, and the same formidable aspect was still presented to us. If there are persons among us who will rest upon conjecture rather than experience, we must earnestly entreat them to reflect that the enormous expence of war is a price too high to pay for their pleasure of conjecturing.

The only remaining chance to which it seems possible that the war advocates can look for better terms of peace than may now be obtained, is a revolution, or a civil war in France. This too is a foundation on which we have most perseveringly built our hopes. This too is a subject on which the lesson of experience is clear and impressive. Has not one revolution followed another? Have we not still fancied that the next would be in favour of our expectations? Have we not still been disappointed? Is it likely that France, which, in

the utmost turbulence of her furious and distract-
ed revolution, was so easily united against all foreign aggression, will, after the firm establishment
of a system of law and order, break herself to
pieces that her neighbours may obtain the advantage ? Did not the government of Bonaparte dis-
appoint all our hopes of insurrection in its infancy, when France was not accustomed to it, when
he had done nothing which seemed in any peculiar
degree to entitle him to that elevation, when
among his brother officers he had many rivals
whose merits and whose claims might appear not
inferior to his own, when the great powers of
Europe still surrounded France in a formidable at-
titude, when the fever of change, in short, still
raged in her veins? And are we now desired to
found the most important of our national decisi-
ons upon the chance of insurrections against the
government of Bonaparte, when it is confirmed
by habit, when he has accomplished the most extraordinary events which are on the record of history, when he has covered France with that kind
of glory which is most dear to the heart of a
Frenchman, when the desire of change among
Frenchmen has decidedly given place to the desire
of security, when Bonaparte has had time to remove all the impediments, and establish all the
springs of his clear-sighted and vigilant administ-
tration ?

Astonishing indeed is the levity with which
mankind allow themselves in general to decide
upon national affairs. You shall find a man of
information and influence, who will listen to the

strongest arguments on this subject which you can adduce, who, will not even inquire if these arguments are answerable, and who will only conclude with an oath against Bonaparte, and a declaration that we must nevertheless fight till we have humbled him. Yet this is a speech so extravagant and irrational, that if it were not so common, and did not harmonize with so many of our favourite passions, we could not believe would be uttered by any reasonable creature. Let us consider with due attention what it implies. We are as little able to humble Bonaparte, as Bonaparte is to humble us. There is hardly any human event that is less within the reach of chance than the humiliation of Bonaparte by the prolongation of our hostilities. This is a truth in which all men appear at last to be agreed ; it is so evident that it seems to defy objection. To ask us therefore to fight for the humiliation of Bonaparte, is, according to the practical rules of human conduct, the same thing as asking us to fight for an impossibility ; it is the same thing as if we were desired to fight till we could make the vines of France grow spontaneously on the mountains of Scotland. Now did they only urge us to let our beards grow till this important event should be accomplished, and were they numerous and powerful enough to set the fashion, we might comply without much indignation. But when they require us to submit to the enormous and destructive consumption of war, when they require us to take the fund destined annually to increase the national produce, and support national happiness; nay to diminish

3

annually the fund of production, to dwindle away
the strength of our country, and spread poverty
and wretchedness among our countrymen, and all
this for an object, on account of which it would
be irrational to require us to submit to the most
trifling permanent inconvenience: no language
can express the absurdity of the proposition.

It lessens not the absurdity to say that we shall
not be in a satisfactory situation during peace.
Because we cannot be as well as we wish, must
we therefore resolve to be as ill as we can be?
This is a favourite plea of the advocates of war;
yet it is the same with that of the drunkard, who,
full of disease by his intemperance, was advised
by his physicians to abstain from drink. Shall I
then, Doctor, cried he, be as well and vigorous
as ever I was? No, said the physician, but you
will be much better than you are now. Oh!
then, said the drunkard, a curse upon temper-
ance! A short life and a merry! This is an exact
parallel to the language of those who reply to all
your remonstrances respecting war, with an oath
against Bonaparte, and a decision that war must
continue, however unavailing, and however expensive. What possible weight, in the delibera-
tions of any rational man, ought it to have in the
question of peace, that peace will not be so happy
a condition as we could wish, when it is absolutely certain that by continuing the war we cannot make it better? If we can do any thing to
render peace a happier condition, let us by all
means do it. But what can induce you to urge a
continuance in that which has no tendency to ren-

K

der that condition better? If a man is in disease, and if by wasting half his substance on physicians he can effect a cure, advise him by all means to persevere: but if, by fifteen years experience, and from a thorough knowledge of his distemper, it is perfectly evident that the physicians can do him no good, and that his restoration must be the slow result of time, if in these circumstances you advise him to waste the other half of his substance upon the Doctors, you resemble exactly the present advocates for the continuance of war.

Numerous, however, as are the subjects of wonder in the opposition to peace, nothing can excite more amazement than that any persons should be found so inconsiderate, and so transported by their passions, as to maintain seriously that war is at present a more desirable situation for us than peace. How differently do men determine concerning their own interests and those of their country! On the side of war, the evil is enormous, clear, certain. No one disputes that war is the greatest calamity with which a nation can be visited. In our case, the waste of the annual produce, the inroad upon the means of national prosperity, and national happiness, is extravagant beyond all former example. Such is the terrible weight placed in the one scale. In the other scale are placed such words as these; " Bonaparte's desire to subdue this country is inextinguishable; he is an artful man, and only desires peace the more effectually to accomplish his purpose." Thus, to balance all the unspeakable mischiefs of war, we have only some vague and conjectural fears! For some vague and conjectural fears we are called upon to endure these unspeakable evils, not for one year, not for two years, not for ten years, but for the life-time of Bonaparte; nay for an endless time, till something which we can neither foresee nor conjecture, shall happen in France, to allay our apprehensions! Is it possible that the mightiest interests of a nation can hang in suspense upon the determination of such a point as this?

Of such infinite importance, however, is this question, that unreal as any argument founded upon these fears appears to be, we will yet examine them with the utmost attention of which we are capable. In the first place we will allow all the premises of our antagonists, however assumed, all their suppositions, however gratuitous; we will yet deny that their conclusion is supported even by a shadow of proof; that it has in its favour so much as a remote probability. They assume that Bonaparte can never cease to plot the ruin of this country; they assume, that he desires peace in order to accomplish that ruin. Let us allow it; and only beg them with the utmost earnestness, as they value the dearest interests of their country, and the happiness of the great body of their countrymen, above their own prejudices and passions, to consider carefully what really ensues. Does it follow that because Bonaparte *desires* to ruin this country, he will yet *be able* to ruin it? He *desires* to ruin it in war surely as much as in peace. Has he been able to ruin it in war? Let him desire to ruin it in peace as much as he pleases, will that *desire* effectuate his purpose? It is a fact which would not be credible if we did not see it, that a great part of our countrymen seriously argue upon the supposition, that, because Bonaparte *desires* to ruin our country in peace, he will therefore *be able* to ruin it. They attempt not to demonstrate to us *how* he will be able. They assume the desire, and seem to think that the execution must follow as an undeniable conclusion. We beg them, however, to exhibit the proof. This is a question on which interests too momentous depend, to be determined by the unbridled licence of supposition.

What means does peace put into the hands of Bonaparte to ruin this country? None; absolutely none. Do not the advocates of war reflect that what renders a country secure in peace is its ability to carry on war; that what renders a country, on the other hand, insecure in peace, is its inability to carry on war? But we have confessedly the power to carry on war; therefore we are perfectly secure in making a peace.

Remarkable are the contrarieties of the human mind. It is in fact a pride, very ill understood, that is at the bottom of the greater part of our aversion to peace, yet the only humiliating confession of inferiority which any one has ever made, is that of those who are afraid to make peace on account of their apprehensions of the power of Bonaparte. Those are the men whose hearts fail them, and who despair of the power of their country. Wherever two countries are completely a match for one another, a peace made on equal terms cannot possibly render the one more preponderant than the other. Where one country is completely a match for another, it can boldly say, I am no more afraid to try with you the relations of peace than the relations of war. I prefer peace to war with all my neighbours. If you mean me well, I am desirous to meet you with corresponding sentiments. If you mean me ill, I am still able to meet and to baffle your malignity. Therefore you will always find me ready to close with you on any reasonable proposals of peace. When a man is conscious of being equal to his antagonist, he can afford to let him place himself in any fair position : when he is afraid that he is inferior, and thinks that in one position he has rather a greater advantage than in another, ne stickles violently to retain that position, and by this very circumstance often loses the day. To say that we are a match for France in war, but not a match for her in peace, is to say that we are only half a match for her. Those among us whose opinion of their country has sunk so low, take counsel from their own timidity, not from a knowledge of their country. They are impressed with a mere habit of apprehending danger from France, not actuated by a careful and rational consideration of the circumstances of the case. These afford the firmest grounds for erect and manly conclusions. The man, who can appreciate the advantages of this country, may with the utmost confidence pronounce her as able to guard against the designs of France in peace as in war; as so completely independent of the power of France, that she can assume with her the relations either of war or of peace, and find herself equally secure in either situation.

In what respect, let us ask our timorous friends, do they expect that the weakness of this country, and the power of France, will shew themselves in the time of peace? Let us suppose that the terms of peace have once been settled, and then let us endeavour to imagine in what way it is possible for Bonaparte to injure us. Will he prepare in secret the means of invasion, and come upon us unawares, like a thief in the night? This is the first, and the greatest of the dangers with which we can be threatened from France. But we may surely take it for granted that this danger, as it regards a time of peace, makes a feeble impression on the minds even of the most timid. In fact it is so seldom urged, that we may be sure it is held in low account. It would, indeed, be an ignorance truly lamentable, to suppose that preparations adequate to the invasion of England could, in a time of peace, be made in secret. Such preparations are not a trifle. Thay cannot be begun, carried on, and ended in an hour. In a time of peace, intercourse is free and rapid. Europe would ring with the noise of such preparations from one corner to the other, before they could be half accomplished. We have no occasion, on this score, to keep our suspicions awake. We might remain in perfect security till we receive intelligence of the fact from Constantinople. The concentration of such a number of troops as

would be required, the conveyance to Boulogne
of the magazines adequate to such an undertaking,
the vast repairs which already must be demanded
to the perishable craft of which the flotilla is
composed, all this would cause in France such a
scene of operation, as would excite the utmost
surprise and agitation throughout Europe. Nor
is any of these the most remarkable circumstance.
We know how long and carefully the men were
exercised in the management of the boats, and
in the service of embarking and landing when
this project was last in agitation. Without much
practice of the same kind renewed, the expedition
could scarcely be undertaken with less than the
prospect of ruin. These extraordinary circum
stances duly weighed, remove completely the fear
of a sudden invasion in the time of peace, prove
indeed the attempt to be so great an absurdity that
it is unreasonable to suppose it could ever be
meditated. A still more important consideration
to the same purpose yet remains to be weighed.
The attempt, supposing it to be made with every
probable advantage, would as certainly be baffled
in a time of peace as in a time of war. What is
the main prop on which our minds have all along
supported themselves in the prospect of invasion?
What is the great object of dread by which Bonaparte has been deterred from executing his project? The determined and unconquerable hos-
tility of our population. Bonaparte has many
times triumphed over a standing army as good as
ours; but he never yet encountered a population
like ours; and of this he and those about him

are thoroughly aware. They are not ignorant
how much their progress has been aided by the
apathy of the people in the countries which they
have subdued. They are not ignorant how impossible it is, not perhaps to overrun, but certainly to subdue a great country, where the population is firmly united, and animated with the
spirit of men who have a country to lose,
animated with the spirit which they expect
to meet in this country. This spirit they would
find invigorated and renewed in a season of
peace, and raised to the highest pitch of ardour
and determination by the unparalleled atrocity of
a treacherous attack in the bosom of peace. The
greatest body of men which Bonaparte, by the
most favourable calculation, can be supposed capable of conveying to our shores, is 50,000 or
60,000 men. But an army approaching to this
amount would not be very heavily felt as a peace
establishment, at a time when all our garrisons
abroad might be reduced to a very slender com-
plement. As far as the protection from our navy
goes, it may, with the utmost ease, be rendered
more complete in the time of peace than in the
time of war. As the great quantity of small
vessels which are at present employed in protect-
ing our trade from privateers will then be dis-
engaged, a much greater number of them, (the
fittest of all kinds of marine for committing
havoc on the flotilla) than was ever in the hottest
time of alarm opposed to it, may, at a very small
expence, be kept in such a state of preparation,

that they could, in the time necessary to bring the flotilla out of the harbour of Boulogne, be sailed to the coast of France to attack it. Enough then, and much more than enough, appears to demonstrate that there is nothing in the chance of invasion that renders peace formidable. But if the fear of invasion in the time of peace be something so very insignificant, surely to undergo the certain consumption of a wide-wasting war, for so trivial an object, would be a strange management of national affairs.

If then the most eager votary of war would not advise the election of its stupendous evils for the evanescent danger of invasion, what other hostile project on the part of Bonaparte is sufficient to counterbalance them ? The article which presents itself as next in magnitude in our budget of apprehension, is the creation of a French navy in the time of peace. The advocates for war are fond of making suppositions. They suppose that if we continue the war a little longer, Bonaparte in the mean time may die, or a confederacy of European princes may rise against him, or a rebellion may break out in France ; any one of which events would enable us to terminate the war with advantage. Now the creation of a fleet to match ours, even Bonaparte, and in a moment too of exaggeration, allowed would require ten years. We then request these gentlemen to make use of one of their own suppositions, and they will see that the naval preparations of Bonaparte will thus become quite harmless before the time of their completion ; while we, in all the intervening years, may be enjoying the un-speakable blessings of peace.

If nothing were requisite to the creation of a fleet but the building of ships, it might be possible with all the resources of France to have, in twenty years, a fleet equal to ours. But if the ships of a fleet are merely the body without the soul, unless Bonaparte has the means of providing something much more valuable than the body, he will only build ships, as hitherto he has done, for the increase of the British navy. But our antagonists will assume that Bonaparte can provide sailors as well as ships in twenty years. Sailors, however, are not made by carpenters just as ships are. Austria will desire to make soldiers as earnestly as Bonaparte will desire to make sailors. If we allow that she will succeed as well, and that she will have an army ready to cope with that of Bonaparte, as soon as Bonaparte can have a fleet ready to cope with ours, here is a complete counterbalance prepared. We shall never have any thing serious to dread from the fleet of France, when Austria has an army perfectly equal to the armies of France. If we say there is something in the circumstances of Austria which will not permit her to form an army equally efficient with that of France, we may with infinitely stronger reason say that there is, in the circumstances of France, what must completely prevent her from forming a body of sailors equal to ours. Austria has a population not much inferior to that of France; the Austrians are a warlike people; the Austrian government is a military government as well as that of France; and in the powers of nature the Austrian territory yields not to the French. But France has no maritime population. She wants therefore the very circumstance on which the life and soul of a fleet depends. This is a point which our antagonists get over by their usual power of supposing. But if we can prove to them that the circumstances and situation of France necessarily prevent her from having a maritime population worthy of being compared with ours, they must then by compulsion allow that France can never have a fleet capable of contending with ours.

It is fortunate that a point on which so much of the stress of this important argument is placed by the advocates of war, seems capable of being determined by proofs uncommonly strong. A maritime population can only be supported by a maritime trade. This is a proposition of intuitive certainty. It does not admit of a question. But France never can have a great maritime trade. Her situation absolutely precludes it. The situation of Great Britain, on the other hand, by necessary causes, creates a great maritime trade. While she has any degree of prosperity she never can be without it. Of the circumference, or bounding line of France, about three-fourths is inland, and only one-fourth sea shore. Great Britain being entirely bounded by the ocean, cannot send an ounce of goods to a foreign country but by means of her sailors. Every part of her foreign commerce serves to create maritime population. But France from three-fourths of her circumference transmits by land the goods which she sells to her neighbours. It is remarkable that the countries which are connected with France by land, are the different countries of Europe; that she is not connected by the ocean with one rich and cultivated country, but Great Britain alone. It is evident, therefore, that supposing France to become a manufacturing country, by far the greatest part of her goods will go to the countries which more immediately surround her, by the great roads, canals, and navigable rivers of Europe, and will not give occasion to the maintenance of even a single sailor. It is worthy too of particular observation that the sea by which France is connected with some of the countries of Europe, is an inland sea, smooth, and tranquil, and totally unfit to form sailors qualified to contend with the hardy, daring, and dexterous sons of the ocean. It is indeed curious to contemplate in what manner this sea must contribute to preclude France from ever being the mistress of a maritime population. It connects her immediately with three quarters of the globe; with some of the richest parts of Europe, Asia, and Africa. It thus opens to her a scope for a boundless commerce at her door. On the shores of the Mediterranean she can trade with advantages peculiarly her own. It will always be much more for the interest of her people to trade with countries where they have advantages over all rivals, than with countries where these rivals have advantages over them. Let France, therefore, become a manufacturing and commercial country to any extent conceivable, her commerce will always be chiefly absorbed by the countries contiguous to her by land, or connected with her by the Mediterranean sea. Great Britain, on the other hand, can trade with no country upon earth, but by means of the ocean. Nor is this, probably, the most remarkable difference in her situation compared with that of France. A very great proportion of the home trade of Great Britain is carried on by the sea. A very insignificant portion of the trade of France can ever be carried on by that means. By reason of the insular situation of Great Britain, every part of it is pretty near the sea. Whenever goods, therefore, have to be transported from one place to another, at any considerable distance, it is always best to send them to the nearest sea-port, and ship them to the sea-port most contiguous to the place to which they are destined. Thus the goods of Manchester are sent to Liverpool, and thence conveyed by sea to London. It is a very small portion of France, however, that is near the sea ; and therefore it is but a very small part of her home trade that can be carried on by sea. The small portion of goods which may be supplied from one place to another of a narrow slip of coast along her western frontier, is all the coasting trade she can ever possess. The immense supplies which are afforded from one part to another of her vast interior, must be all by inland carriage. The whole intercourse, on the other hand, in heavy goods between the distant parts of Great Britain, is a coasting trade. The proportion which the shipping employed in that trade bears to that in the aggregate trade of the nation is already very great, and as the parts of the country which are most distant from the centre of improvement advance, it is a trade which must greatly increase. Such are the causes, in the physical, and unalterable circumstances of the two countries, which must for ever prevent France from having any considerable maritime population, and must at all times secure a great maritime population in Great Britain. But if France can never have a considerable maritime population, and Britain must always have a great one, how is it possible that France can ever have a fleet which ought to be compared with that of Britain? France, besides, has always been a country bare of capital. After the expensive wars she has recently carried on, and the destruction occasioned by her revolution, she must, of necessity, be at present more deficient in capital than formerly. But whenever a country is deficient in capital, all that she makes is for a long time absorbed in her agriculture, and manufactures for home consumption; nor is it till after great accumulation, the slow offspring of time, that she has any thing to spare for foreign commerce; maritime commerce, therefore, in France, or the creation of a maritime population, are effects of a peace which there is not a shadow of reason to dread. By consequence the danger of a fleet which can be formidable to ours, is imaginary.

It thus appears that the apprehensions of those among us who distrust the power of their country are altogether unfounded. The proof seems to be as complete, as the general nature of human affairs admits, that Bonaparte can neither openly subdue, nor secretly undermine our independence in the time of peace. The danger of invasion is reduced to nothing; the creation of a navy comparable to ours is an impossibility; the sphere of French commerce, when her commerce begins, is totally different from the British? when she becomes rich and industrious she will widen the European market, not contract it; she will create new scope for the British commerce, not annihilate the old. This is the irresistible nature of things, which no human power can controul. The government of France may prevent her from having any commerce, but no government can make commerce proceed in opposition to its own laws. A tyrant can make the blood cease to circulate in any of his subjects, but he cannot make it circulate in a course different from that which the laws of nature have ordained. It thus appears that we may put an end to the destructive consumption of war, without even the smallest risk. But so vast are the evils of war, and so mighty are the blessings of peace, that even a great risk would be wisely encountered for the attainment of the one, and deliverance from the other. How extraordinary then would be the impolicy of struggling without end in the present unavailing, and expensive contest?

Among the people, however, who have prejudices against peace, there are some, more reasonable than others, who say that peace will deduct but little from the expence of the war; that were the peace which we should have, like an ordinary peace, when our naval and military establishments would be reduced, they would then be advocates for peace, as the blessings of such a peace would, in their apprehension, overbalance its risks; but as we must keep up our peace establishment to nearly the level of war, all that we should gain is hardly worth the trouble of change. The very circumstance on which the stress of this objection rests, is the circumstance which renders the reflecting mind most anxious to accelerate the period of peace. Such is the state of irritation and alarm in which we are placed with regard to France, that let peace happen when it will, we shall still imagine at first that we have occasion for a burthensome establishment. Time would gradually dispel our jealousies, on both sides; the inconvenience of such establishments would daily undermine them in both countries; and in the course of three or four years we should, in all probability, find them reduced to a pretty reasonable magnitude. But if we continue warring, for twenty years, the same objection to peace will still exist; the same course would still remain to be run. It is not in war that our mutual irritation and jealousies can subside. There is no probability that at the end of twenty years warring, France would to us be less formidable than she is at present. We should at the end of twenty years, then, have the same occasion for a large peace establishment as we have now; and as we can only hope to be delivered from this evil by the salutary operation of peace, the sooner peace arrives the more happy is the event. As it is a burthen which is sure to be attached to the first peace which we shall make, however distant, we shall only render ourselves the less able to bear it, by undergoing still longer the exhaustion of war.

Such is the view which presents itself of the policy of peace, even on the supposition that the desire of Bonaparte for our destruction is inextinguishable, even if we knew by a revelation from heaven that Bonaparte had sworn our ruin, and would never desist from his purpose, still we might fearlessly contract a peace, and defy his malignity; still it would be our wisdom to make peace, and maintain it with vigilance, temper, and constancy. This would be our most effectual course to defeat his plans. This view of the question I have been anxious to present fully, because our resentments run so very high against our enemy, that his insatiable malignity is a point which we can seldom permit to be doubted. As this argument, however, is finished, and is entirely independent of what follows, we may offer a few considerations towards the forming an estimate of the disposition of Bonaparte in respect to a peace. They may do some good, and can hardly do any harm, except that, perhaps, of drawing upon the author the charge of some zealot, that he has a desire for the ruin of his country. But this is a charge which is now so common, and has been laid upon so many good men, that he cannot feel it very heavily.

L

In the first place we can have no manner of doubt that Bonaparte would be very well pleased to subdue us, could that event be easily accomplished. We cannot help, too, perceiving certain circumstances in his situation which tend to make this desire stronger than is usual between belligerent countries. We have raised up against him extraordinary hostilities; he knows our hatred of him is intense; we are the nation which can oppose the chief obstructions to his designs. Thus far reason conducts us in supposing hostile intentions in the breast of Bonaparte; but not one step farther. If we suppose that he cannot make a distinction between what is possible, and what is impossible; if we suppose he cannot make a distinction between such desires as he can safely endeavour to gratify, and such as he cannot endeavour to gratify without a greater chance of evil than good, we draw our conclusions neither from the laws of human nature, nor from a knowledge of Bonaparte. Now Great-Britain, as appears from evidence much stronger than can in general be obtained on such subjects, it is impossible for France to subdue. Of this Bonaparte is much more completely aware than those of our countrymen who are so desperately afraid to make peace. Bonaparte, however, would be little an object of dread, were he foolish enough to endeavour to compass an impossibility. The monarch who threw chains into the ocean because it destroyed his boats, was easily conquered. But, if it be impossible, or any thing near impossible, to subjugate Britain, the slightest reflection must convince Bonaparte, that the chance of evil to him is much greater than the chance of good in making any attempt to subdue it. Now it is one of the laws of human nature that a man always acquiesces in an impossibility, or any thing so difficult, that in his case it may be regarded as an impossibility. This is exemplified in the conduct of the most impetuous and wilful of mankind. Even Alexander the Great stopt short in the midst of the conquest of India, on which his heart seemed to be more strongly bent than on any other of his undertakings, when the difficulties of the country, and the reluctance of his army presented obstacles which he found it would be dangerous to encounter. This has been exemplified in a still more striking manner in the conduct of Bonaparte. At the moment when we enraged him so much by terminating the peace of Amiens, who doubts that his desire to subdue this country was then at its height? Such was at that time the opinion, almost universally entertained by us, of his impetuosity and resentment, that we assured ourselves he would make the invasion with headlong fury before the expiration of many months. Yet we saw him consume two whole years in preparation, and even after his preparations were made, by the exercise of a little more reflection, abandon the enterprise. Thus, in time of war, we have experimental proof that Bonaparte acquiesces in the impossibility of subduing this country. But we have proved that the impossibility is equal; nay greater, of subduing it in time of peace. There is the highest reason surely to conclude that Bonaparte will acquiesce in the one impossibility as well as the other. It is a conclusion founded upon the most steady and certain principle, from which we can reason concerning the actions of man; that a very clear, and very important interest must always determine his choice. This is the principle from which we conclude, that Bonaparte desires peace with this country, and that he will not desire to break it. We never can have a stronger security for the sincerity of the counter party in any treaty of peace.

To this powerful evidence what have our antagonists to offer in reply? They tell us, 'that 'Bonaparte is ambitious, and that ambition is 'insatiable.' Thus, by a mere common place, of the most vague, and unmeaning class, they would have us set aside evidence, founded upon the most invariable laws of human nature. Is not every passion insatiable, just as much as ambition is? Has not the moralist in all ages warned us against the insatiable nature of passion in general? Avarice, for example, is universally described as insatiable. The more the avaricious man has, the more he desires. But does this hinder him from distinguishing between the modes of gratifying this desire; from perceiving that by certain modes, he may gratify it with safety, by other modes, if he attempts them, he will incur mischief? Does the insatiable nature of avarice urge the avaricious man to try impudently to wrest his money from another man, or secretly to purloin it, when he knows that both his open, and his secret schemes will certainly be disappointed; and that he himself will be punished for the attempt? Does the insatiable nature of avarice make, in general, the avaricious man either robber or thief? Why? because the apparent evil of such undertakings is greater than the probable good. This is precisely the reasoning which we suppose to have an influence upon Bonaparte. We only suppose him to yield to the common, and strongest impulses of human nature. Nay more, all that we suppose him to do, is only to consult with the most ordinary prudence, the interests of that ambition itself, by which our controvertists suppose him to be entirely governed. The risk which he runs in attempting the subjugation of Britain, is all against his ambition. Nothing else, which can easily happen to him, would contribute so effectually to lessen, nay, to anihilate his power, as a failure in this momentous undertaking. As its failure, by every rule of human calculation, seems to be certain; unless Bonaparte means the death-blow to his ambition, he cannot be supposed to meditate so dangerous and hopeless a project.

Were we not resolved to interpret every thing according to our passions, the desire which Bonaparte has so often manifested to conclude a peace with Britain, could not have failed to make a strong impression. The clear certainty, that he can possess no advantage over us in peace, any more than in war, is the strongest proof which can be imagined, that he desires peace for the sake of peace, and its own fair and mutual advantages. In fact, if we examine the matter candidly, we shall perceive that the conclusion of peace is now almost the only thing which can add to the glory of Bonaparte, and the stability of his power. Whatever conquest can atchieve for him is done. From no external power has he now any attempt to fear, which can shake his throne. He has gratified Frenchmen to their hearts content with military renown, and placed himself infinitely above his late rivals. To give to Frenchmen the blessings of peace, and establish an interest in their gratitude, is all that now remains for him, to place his power on as firm a basis, as any newly acquired supremacy seems capable of attaining. Besides, Bonaparte now regards the empire of France as his, and as the patrimony of his family. He has, therefore, a natural interest in its prosperity. He regards its prosperity as his prosperity. It is not as when he was a mere adventurer, struggling to have the ascendency, and careless how much for that purpose he wasted a country, with which his connection at that time was very loose. But he sees, that war is inconsistent with her prosperity; that exhausted as she is, she has the most unspeakable need of the restorative blessings of peace. Is it then wonderful that he should wish for it? Is it extraordinary that he should desire an event so much calculated to add to the stability of his throne, and to the splendour of his government * ?

The readiness, nay, the forwardness with which Bona-

6

If we recollect the natural pride of the man, how much his unparalleled success has tended to blow it up, how necessary he accounts it not to lower his dignity with a country which has sought industriously for occasions to affront him, we shall be astonished at the lengths he has gone for the attainment of peace. I could earnestly wish, that every one who allows himself to talk upon this subject, and still more, every one whose sen-

parte has on various, and very extraordinary occasions, acceded to proposals of peace, is one of not the least remarkable circumstances in his career. Let us just reflect on some of them. In the spring of 1797, he had advanced into the heart of Austria at the head of 80,000 men; a force which the Austrians had no means of opposing. Instead of pushing forward to the capital, he proposed terms of peace; the Austrians asked an armistice; and though it was entirely adverse to him, as it enabled the Austrians to concentrate their remaining forces, he consented to it, and the preliminaries of Leoben were signed.—In the next war, after the decisive victory of Hohenlinden, he offered to treat with the Emperor, on nearly the same terms as before.—Having overthrown an Austrian force of nearly 80,000 men at Ulm, he sent an urgent message to the Emperor Francis to make peace.—After the battle of Austerlitz, when Austria lay at his mercy, he immediately welcomed the proposals of the Emperor.—It appears from the official paper in the Moniteur, of 7th January, 1808, that a word from Lord Lauderdale, would have stopped the fatal march against Prussia in 1806. Bonaparte's letter from Genoa urged the King of Prussia to make peace before the battle of Jena, and we now find, that he twice offered him a separate peace after that irretrievable disaster.—Towards this country, his declarations have uniformly, during the last four years, been pacific. In January, 1805, he made an overture for negociation; we refused it, and stirred up the Continent against him. In the spring of 1806, after conquering Austria, his language to his senate was; " I desire peace with " England; no resentments of mine shall retard it."

timents will have any influence upon the national decision, would read with attention the collection of papers connected with the late negotiation, which was published by our own government. As any analysis of these important documents, would here occupy too large a space, I am happy to be able to refer to a tract, which I suppose is in the hands of most of my readers, and in which that analysis is exhibited in the most satisfactory form, The " Inquiry into the state of the British West Indies," by Mr. Lowe*. It is not so much the favourable terms here offered to us, as the tone of the negotiation, which is the wonderful circumstance. On our side appear the utmost haughtiness and impatience. At every untoward incident were we for putting an end to the negotiation instantly; demanded our passports; and seemed to think it condescension to say to the French negociator, that we would meet him again upon the business†. The French even submitted to court us not to break off the negotiation; and offered such terms, as we should not beforehand have easily believed we

* See that work from p. 91 to p. 131. See also the supplement to the 3d edit. of the same work.

† Lord Lauderdale, in a letter to his government, giving an account of one of the last conferences he had with Mons. Champagny, thus writes; " After strong expressions of mu-" tual regard, he attended me to the outer room, where he " again proposed a renewal of our conferences, in case his go-" vernment should give him new instructions. My answer " was, that I had no choice in immediately applying for pass-" ports; but that, as long as I remained in this country, *I* " *never would refuse to see him*." See official papers.

could obtain. Hanover, Malta, the Cape of Good Hope, Pondicherry, Tobago, were all to be resigned. But on this circumstance, we have no occasion now to dwell, since his Majesty has declared, in his answer to the declaration of the Emperor of Russia, dated at Westminster, December 18th, 1807, *that the terms which were offered to Great Britain, were perfectly satisfactory, and that it was on account of the interests of Russia solely, that the negotiation was broken off.* This averment on the part of an administration, composed of the leading persons in the party which is most averse to peace, is in the highest degree important. " The Emperor of Russia," says this royal declaration, " cannot fail " to remember, that the last negotiation between " Great Britain and France was broken off, upon " points immediately affecting, not his Majesty's " own interests, but those of his imperial ally." This is a public, deliberate, solemn declaration, before all Europe, that Great Britain had nothing to fear from France, in a peace concluded upon the terms which were offered in the late negotiation, that the interests of Great Britain were completely secured by those terms; that the negotiation did not break off upon points affecting the interests of his Britannic Majesty. But if it was safe for Great Britain to make peace upon those terms then, it is safe, for her to make peace upon similar terms now. The question then about the advantage of a peace is decided by the authority of government itself; for there is not a doubt, that the same terms may now be obtained.

The only new circumstance which it might have been feared would create materials of controversy, was the dispute about our maritime claims. But in the remarks which have been recently published in the Moniteur, upon that very paper which I have quoted above, Bonaparte has volunteered, in removing this difficulty per advance. He has declared, that our maritime claims will never come in question in the negotiation for peace. If then we may have the same terms of peace, which were offered to us in the negotiation conducted by Lords Yarmouth and Lauderdale, if those terms completely secured the interests of Great Britain, and if the negotiation was broken off upon questions solely touching the interests of Russia, what can hinder us from accepting of those terms now, when Russia has made a peace for herself?

THE END.

C. and R. Baldwin, Printers,
New Bridge-Street, London.